FLORA MAC DONALD

FLORA MACDONALD
IN AMERICA

with a

Brief Sketch of Her Life and Adventures

by

J.P. MACLEAN, Ph.D.

Life Member Gaelic Society of Glasgow, and Clan MacLean Association of Glasgow; Corresponding Member Davenport Academy of Sciences, and Western Reserve Historical Society; Author of History of Clan MacLean, Scotch Highlanders in America, Antiquity of Man, the Mound Builders, Mastodon, Mammoth and Man, Norse Discovery of America, Fingal's Cave, Introduction Study of Nature Worship, Life of Richard Mc-Nemar, Bibliography of Shaker Literature, Etc.

'Mid the pomp of huge London her heart still was yearning
For her home in the corrie, the crag, and the glen;
Though fair be the daughters of England, the fairest
And stateliest walks in the land of the Ben.

SCOTPRESS
Morgantown, West Virginia
1984

First published 1909 by A.W. McLean

Reprinted 1984 by SCOTPRESS
P.O. Box 778
Morgantown, West Virginia

ISBN 0-912951-20-6

To

ANGUS WILTON McLEAN, Esq.

of

LUMBERTON, NORTH CAROLINA

Whose ancestors
bore an important part in the scenes wherein

Flora MacDonald

was a chief actor in North Carolina
and who takes a deep interest in all things pertaining
to that event, as well as those relating to the Highlands
of Scotland and his own distinguished clan, besides
being busily engaged in the practice of law
and the development of the natural resources of his native State, this
volume is respectfully
dedicated by

THE AUTHOR

The Lament of Flora MacDonald

Far over yon hills of the heather so green,
   And down by the corrie that sings to the sea,
The bonnie young Flora sat sighing her lane,
   The dew on her plaid, and the tear in her e'e.
She looked at a boat with the breezes that swung
   Away on the wave, like a bird of the main;
And aye as it lessened, she sighed and she sung,
   "Farewell to the lad I shall ne'er see again!
Farewell to my hero, the gallant and young!
   Farewell to the lad I shall ne'er see again.

"The moorcock that crows on the brow of Ben-Connal,
   He kens o' his bed in a sweet mossy hame,
The eagle that soars o'er the cliffs o' Clan-Ronald,
   Unawed and unhunted, his eyrie can claim,
The solan can sleep on his shelf of the shore,
   The cormorant roost on his rock of the sea;
But, oh! there is ane whose hard fate I deplore;
   Nor house, ha', nor hame, in his country has he.
The conflict is past, and our name is no more:
   There's naught left but sorrow for Scotland and me.

"The target is torn from the arms of the just,
The helmet is cleft on the brow of the brave,
The claymore forever in darkness must rust,
   But red is the sword of the stranger and slave;
The hoof of the horse, and the foot of the proud
   Have trode o'er the plumes on the bonnet of blue.
Why slept the red bolt in the breast of the cloud,
   When tyranny reveled in blood of the true?
Farewell, my young hero, the gallant and good,
   The crown of thy fathers is torn from thy brow."

                    —James Hogg.

Table of Contents

CHAPTER I.

CAVE IN SKYE OCCUPIED BY PRINCE CHARLES JUST BEFORE
LEAVING FOR RAASAY

FLORA MAC DONALD
(From Allan Ramsay's Painting from Life)

Flora MacDonald in America

CHAPTER I.

INTRODUCTORY NOTE.

Flora MacDonald needs no introduction to all true lovers of Highland Scotch history. It is superfluous to pass an eulogium on her character, or sing her praises. She lives, and will continue to live in the hearts of all who are able to appreciate disinterested heroism of an exalted type. Her countrymen had just been defeated while engaged in the greatest act of chivalry the world had ever witnessed. It was befitting that a woman of true nobility of character should be called on to bear a part, daring, heroic, and romantic. Her character has been extolled; her praises embalmed in song; her heroism depicted as an example to be imitated, and her patriotism to be admired. Withal, a person to be loved for her womanly virtues, which must be regarded as a just pattern of excellence.

The admiration and esteem for Flora MacDonald are largely due to an act on her part which took place between June 26 and 30, 1746, when, at a critical period, she saved Prince Charles Edward from falling into the hands of his enemies. Even a stranger story remains here to be told. Her act at the age of twenty-four, embellished in story and song, has long overshadowed a greater and more deliberate heroism performed at the ripe age of fifty-four. This has been passed over, or else referred to only incidentally. Flora MacDonald was a greater power and a more commanding figure during her residence in America than when she displayed her heroism by saving the life of him who brought countless woes upon her countrymen and hurled many valiant souls down to destruction. Yet how little is known of Flora MacDonald in America! The fugitive articles and biographical notices of her in the press of her native country betray almost a total ignorance on the subject. Even her biography, written by her granddaughter, Mrs. Flora Frances Wilde, extending to nearly four hundred pages, two-thirds of which is pure fiction, passes over this interesting period with a notice of less than four pages. The "Life of Flora Mac-Donald," written by Rev. Alexander Macgregor, a more conscientious and painstaking biographer, contains but five pages relating to her sojourn in America.

Having seen no satisfactory account of Flora MacDonald's life in North Carolina, I was moved to make a thorough investigation, the result of which I published in the *Celtic Monthly,* Glasgow, for the year 1900. By request of the editor of the *American Monthly Magazine,* I abridged the account, and the same appears in the issue of that journal for August, 1900. Then I dismissed the subject from my mind with no thought of ever pursuing it again.

By special invitation, on the morning of February 20, 1909, I entered the hospitable mansion of Hon. Angus W. McLean, Lumberton, North Carolina, to pay him a visit. Within less than an hour after my appearance, complete arrangements had been entered into, by which I was to rewrite my production on Flora MacDonald, and Mr. McLean was to finance the enterprise. I had no hesitancy on entering into the compact, because I knew that North Carolina contained a very large Highland Scotch population, where the name of Flora MacDonald is venerated, to say nothing of a similar people scattered throughout the various States of the Union, besides the same race in Canada. As these people take a just pride in their ancestry it was safe to infer that the publication would receive a hearty welcome.

It was but a natural consequence that Mr. McLean should be specially interested in Flora MacDonald. His great-grandfather, John MacLean, emigrated from the Isle of Mull to North Carolina, and the clan of MacLean, of that period, was still a strong partisan of the House of Stuart. Besides this, Mr. McLean's great-grandfather, Colonel James MacQueen, was a grandnephew of the heroine of this story, and came to North Carolina, from the Isle of Skye, in the year 1765, accompanied by his sisters, Polly, Nepsie, and Isabel. He landed at Wilmington, proceeded up the Cape Fear River to Cross Creek, where he remained for a short time, and then, with his sisters, went to Anson County, and there taught school for several years. He was living in that county when Flora MacDonald came to America, and through his influence Allen and Flora MacDonald were persuaded to leave Cameron's Hill and settle in Anson County. Flora lived for a short time with the MacQueen's before settling at Killiegrey. Just after the close of the Revolution, Colonel MacQueen married Nancy MacRae, and purchased a large tract of land about ten miles south of Maxton, giving his home the name of Queensdale, which it still retains. He was a frequent visitor at Flora MacDonald's, and during her hours of adversity, supplied her with money and looked after her necessities while her husband was a prisoner. When Flora left America for Skye, he again supplied her with money to meet her expenses and pressing obligations. He had been successful in amassing what, at that time, was a large fortune.

It is only fair to state that some points in the narrative I found myself unable to unravel. I notified Mr. McLean, who at once gave his time and energy and succeeded in gaining valuable information, and placed the same at my disposal. I further state the manuscript of this work was not submitted to his inspection, and the contents are wholly on my own responsibility.

Before leaving North Carolina, I set about securing all available information, visited Cross Creek (now Fayetteville), sought out those supposed to have items of interest, and from all, living in different communities, I received the utmost courtesy. To Mr. John MacLean, of Glasgow, Scotland, I am indebted for photos of the monument of Flora MacDonald's grave, and her statue in the city of Inverness. The illustrations of scenes in Skye are taken from Thomas Pennant's *Tour in Scotland and Voyage to the Hebrides,* made in 1772.

The object of this production is not to present the life of Flora MacDonald, but mainly to confine the account to her history as connected with North Carolina, though recognizing the necessity for a brief historical sketch in order that a uniform narrative may be maintained. In presenting this testimony, with the additional facts revealed, it is hoped that the effort will meet the approval of all who are interested in the life and character of the Scottish heroine. If such shall be the result, then I shall feel well repaid for my labor.

Franklin, Ohio, April 6, 1909.

CHAPTER II.

FLORA MACDONALD'S EARLY LIFE.

Flora MacDonald, of the family of Clanranald, a sept of the Clan MacDonald, was born in 1722—month and day not given—in Milton, South Uist, one of the outer Hebrides of Scotland. Patronimically she was designated "Fionnghal nighean Raonuill'ic Aonghais Oig, an Airidh Mhuilinn," or "Flora, the daughter of Ranald, the son of Angus, younger of Milton." Her mother was Marian, daughter of Rev. Angus MacDonald. Flora was the only daughter of the family, but she had two brothers. Her younger brother, Angus, succeeded his father at Milton, while her mother, in 1728, married, for her second husband, Captain Hugh MacDonald of Armadale in Skye. On the removal of the mother to Armadale, Angus felt very reluctant to part with his sister, then six years of age. As the mother and son could not agree, the decision was left to Flora. On being asked if she preferred to go to Skye with her mother, or remain with her brother at Milton, she instantly replied, "I will stay at Milton because I love it. I do not know Skye, and do not care for it. I will therefore remain with Angus until my dear mamma comes back to me." As a child she was precocious, and her behavior so excellent that parents who knew her, in correcting their own children would ask them, "C'uin a bhios sibh cosmhuil ri Fionnghal Nighean Roanuill, an Airidh-Mhuilinn?" or, "When will you resemble Flora of Milton?" She was a particular favorite with all the families of the Isle, especially so with Clanranald (Ranald MacDonald, fifteenth of Clanranald) and his lady, the latter acting toward her more like a mother than a distant relative.

At the age of thirteen Flora entered the family of Clanranald at Ormiclade, and there remained for three years, receiving instruction from a governess retained in the hospitable mansion. In 1739, Lady Clanranald was persuaded by Lady Margaret MacDonald, wife of Sir Alexander MacDonald of the Isles, residing at Monkstadt, in Skye, to send Flora to her, as she and Sir Alexander were desirous that Flora should be educated. Accordingly, in the fall of 1741, she was sent to Edinburgh, and there attended a boarding-school provided for girls, and in that city she stayed continuously for over three years, and attended closely to her education.

On receiving the news of the disastrous defeat of the British at Fontenoy, Sir Alexander determined to leave Edinburgh, with Lady Margaret and Flora, for home. On the third of June, the party went on board the *Brothers* in Leith harbor, and on the evening of the same day set sail. On board was a goodly company, among which was Lord President Forbes of Culloden. After eight days the vessel landed its passengers at Inverness, where Sir Alexander was met by his servants with three horses properly saddled to convey the party to Skye, and after a tiresome journey over bridlepaths, in due time arrived safely at Monkstadt.

Having remained four days at Monkstadt, Flora procured passage for the Long Island, in order to visit her brother at Milton and also Lady Clanranald at Ormiclade. She received a warm reception from her old friends who assembled in order to bid her welcome. So happy was old Clanranald that he addressed his young friend in Gaelic: "Flora, my dear, I rejoice to see your comely face again. You are welcome back to the Isle of your birth, for the household was devoid of joy and gladness since you left it; and even 'Ceolag' itself (the small pianoforte), as if under lamentation, was mute."

CHAPTER III.

FLORA MACDONALD BECOMES FAMOUS.

At the time of the return of Flora MacDonald to her native Isle, almost all of Scotland was in a state of excitement over the rumor that Prince Charles Edward Stuart was about to visit them. The partisans of the House of Stuart who were with Prince Charles kept their friends in the Isles and on the mainland posted regarding the movements and purposes of the young chevalier.

On July 23, 1745, on board the Doutelle, Prince Charles arrived at the Island of Eriska, in the Sound of Barra.

It is foreign to the purpose, in this connection, to enter even into an epitome of the uprising of the Highlanders in 1745, in behalf of the House of Stuart, which ended in the disastrous battle of Culloden, fought on Drummossi Muir, near Inverness, April 16, 1746. That history has been frequently and graphically retold, and all the facts readily accessible to all who may need inquire.

The overthrow of the Highland army was followed by a brutality and inhumanity unequaled in the annals of history, practised under the direct command of the Duke of Cumberland, son of the reigning sovereign. "Rebel hunting," as Cumberland and his lawless soldiery called it, was mercilessly practised in every quarter. Outrages were perpetrated on defenseless women too shocking to be narrated. The duke issued a proclamation denouncing immediate death, by being shot or hanged, against all persons who harbored any of the rebels, or aided them to escape into their mountain recesses. Prince Charles believing that his cause was not hopeless, determined to make his way as quickly as possible to France, in order to use his personal exertions in procuring powerful supplies. Without announcing his intentions he set out upon a westerly course, arriving at Invergary Castle on the seventeenth on his way to the Long Island, where he hoped to find a vessel, whereby he could be conveyed to France. On the twenty-seventh he landed on the Long Island, and his arrival there created great excitement. Soon his situation became desperate, for the English took immediate action for guarding every avenue of escape, and the unfortunate prince learned that a reward of £30,000 had been offered for his apprehension.

During the period above referred to, Flora MacDonald resided principally with the family at Ormiclade. Old Clanranald and Sir Alexander MacDonald sympathized with the existing government, and Flora's feelings were enlisted with those of her chief. The hardships of the prince were rehearsed to her, and her amiable disposition naturally went out to him in his misfortunes, little thinking that soon her good services should be called upon to extricate him from his perilous position.

Suffering, want, and danger rapidly pressed upon the prince. In the hour of dire extremity, Flora MacDonald was appealed to and urged to become his deliverer, as at that time he was in her immediate neighborhood. She was informed of his miserable state; the cold and damp cave in which he was sheltered; his gaunt, haggard, and half-famished appearance; his tattered raiment, and yet hopeful disposition. It required but little persuasion to induce her to comply, for a recital of the prince's condition appealed to her sympathies, and fully realizing that immediate action was necessary, she formed her plans, after listening to the advice of others. She repaired to Milton in order that her brother might be acquainted with her design. On her return from Milton she was seized by a party of militia, and having no passport, was detained prisoner for the night. Early on the following morning her step-father, Captain Hugh MacDonald, in command, found her in the guard-house, which was a small, turf-built hut, roofed with bulrushes. Flora applied to him for a passport for herself, her manservant, an Irish spinning-maid named Betty Burke, and for six of a crew, all destined for Armadale in Skye. On June 26, Flora was conducted to the cave where the prince had taken refuge. As the prince was to impersonate Betty Burke, the proper dress had been provided and brought along. No sooner had the prince been metamorphosed into a tall, awkward, Irish servant than a messenger arrived announcing that Captain Ferguson and Major Allan MacDonald, with troops, had reached Ormiclade, and that Lady MacDonald, who had accompanied

Flora, must hasten home to avoid suspicion. On reaching home she was rigidly and rudely questioned by her military visitors. On the night of June 27, the prince narrowly escaped being taken prisoner. Flora had procured a boat with six oarsmen, and every other necessary, and walked along the shore with Lady Clanranald to a distance of a mile from Clanranald's house, where, according to appointment, the prince (dressed as Betty Burke) and Colonel O'Neale met her. The rain was falling in torrents. To their consternation they saw four armed cutters so close to the shore that they could not get away unobserved by the soldiers on board the boats, and therefore skulked among the rocks till the vessels passed them. In about an hour after, their own boat, concealed in a neighboring creek, with muffled oars, rowed up gently to the spot where it was so anxiously expected. With all possible speed they embarked on their perilous voyage across the Minch to Skye, a distance of nearly forty miles.

The voyage proved to be perilous in the extreme. The whole channel was scoured by armed vessels, making the chances of success exceedingly doubtful. On leaving the shore the weather was calm and serene, and then a moderate breeze sprang up, but the wind was favorable. Within a few hours one of those summer storms, so common in the Isles, unexpectedly came on, the wind blowing terrific gusts, rolling the billows high, and threatening to engulf the frail craft. Then a thunder-storm set in, painfully alarming the party as to their safety. The crew, composed of picked men, excellent seamen and skilled in managing a craft in a storm, was forced to call forth their utmost energies that night to manage the boat amid the raging billows. At break of day the storm moderated, and in the dim distance appeared the lofty headlands of Skye. As the boat approached Waternish, a party of the MacLeod militia stationed there ran to the shore with their guns and leveled them at the boat. The tide being out, the crew, with desperate pulls, forced the boat beyond the reach of the militia, amid a shower of bullets which riddled the sails, cleft the handle of the helm, and grazed a finger of the steersman. The prince stood up and cheered the crew and also endeavored to persuade Flora to remain in the bottom of the boat. This she declined unless he also would seek

DUNVEGAN CASTLE, SKYE
(From Pennant's "Tour in Scotland." Taken in 1772)

such protection. Eventually as the danger increased, both squatted down and so continued until the boat was out of danger.

When once more fairly out at sea, Flora, overcome with the watchfulness and anxiety of the night, fell asleep upon the bottom of the boat. Proceeding on their voyage a few miles to the northward, the boat was put into a cleft, in order to rest and refresh the rowers; but the alarm which their appearance occasioned in a village hard by, obliged them to put to sea again. Finally they landed, on the twenty-ninth, at a place called Kilbride, in the parish of Kilmuir, and within five hundred yards of Monkstadt, the residence of Sir Alexander MacDonald.

Under a shelving rock at Kilbride, at that time, was a cave into which the prince entered. Flora, accompanied by her faithful servant, Niel (father of the celebrated Marshall MacDonald, Duke of Tarentum), repaired at once to Monkstadt. The heroine was at once shown into the drawing-room where she found quite a number in military dress, among whom was Captain John MacLeod, in command of a company of militia stationed two miles distant. MacLeod's language to her was rude and the questions put to her positively uncivil; but she never lost her self-possession, and all her replies were in calm and pleasing words. Her deportment was so fascinating and agreeable throughout that she won the esteem of the officer, and had the honor of being escorted by him to dinner, where she received his most assiduous attentions. Although he had rigidly examined every boat that landed in his vicinity, yet, through the consummate diplomacy of Flora, he neglected that which bore the maiden and her companions.

It was of the utmost importance that Lady MacDonald should be secretly apprised of the situation. This duty devolved upon Alexander MacDonald, of Kingsburgh, factor to Sir Alexander. Although Lady MacDonald was a thorough Jacobite, yet the information greatly alarmed her. It was decided that the prince should at once be removed to Kingsburgh's residence, situated some miles distant on the north shore of Loch Snizort.

Having delayed the company a sufficient length of time for Kingsburgh and the prince to get a good start, Flora arose from the table and announced she should take her departure. Lady MacDonald affected great concern at her short stay and entreated her to prolong it.

Flora, on the other hand, pleaded the necessity of being at home on account of her mother's illness. With great apparent reluctance, Lady MacDonald permitted her young guest to depart.

On the journey Flora, with her servant, Niel, was accompanied by Mrs. MacDonald of Kirkibost and her two servants, all five riding on horseback. They soon overtook the prince, who had thus far walked on the public highway, but was soon to turn off on an unfrequented path across the wild country. Flora, anxious that her fellow-traveler's servants should not see the route of the prince, called upon the party to ride faster; and the two pedestrians were passed at a trot. Mrs. MacDonald's girl perceiving the prince, still in female attire, remarked that she "had never seen such a tall, impudent-looking woman in her life! See," she continued, addressing Flora, "what long strides the jade takes! I dare say she is an Irish woman, or else a man in woman's clothes."

After an uncomfortable day's traveling through the rain, Kingsburgh, Flora, and the prince arrived safely at Kingsburgh House about eleven at night.

The following day Prince Charles, Kingsburgh, and Flora set out on foot for Portree, fourteen miles distant. After pursuing their way a considerable distance, the prince, with Kingsburgh, retired into a wood, where the former exchanged his female attire into a suit consisting of a short coat and waistcoat, a philibeg and short hose, a plaid, a wig, and a bonnet. There the company separated, Kingsburgh to return home, the prince to proceed, accompanied by a little herdboy, and Flora taking a different route for the same place. At Portree the prince took farewell of Flora by saying, "For all that has happened, I hope, madam, we shall meet in St. James yet." He never communicated with her afterwards, nor recognized the obligations due her and the gratitude which he should have expressed, although he lived for forty-two years after the parting in Portree.

There is a tradition, still current among the descendants of Col. James MacQueen, in North Carolina, that Prince Charles, while being piloted by Flora MacDonald, came near being captured at one of their stopping-places, from the manner in which he received peas served in the house where they were stopping. After supper some one suggested

PARTING OF FLORA MAC DONALD AND PRINCE CHARLES
(From "Ascanius; or, the Young Adventurer")

that the peas be shelled for the next day, and all agreed to join in the work. The hostess, in distributing the peas to be shelled, suggested to the other women present to prepare their laps for them. All the women present, except "Bettie Burke," spread their laps, as was the custom, to receive them, while Bettie drew her (his) knees together, man fashion. The incident was observed and remarked at the time and came nearly leading to the detection that Bettie was a man in disguise, only the hurried departure of Flora and her charge preventing detection.

Flora, having parted with the prince at Portree, went to spend a few days with her mother at Armadale, and then took her departure for her brother's residence at Milton.

A mistake was made in allowing the boat which brought the party to Skye to return so soon. Flora did not order it, nor did she command the men to stay. On the return of the boat the men were instantly arrested and examined separately, when all the facts became known.

Having arrived at Milton, Flora took no steps to conceal herself, although aware that she was being diligently sought for, as she was now considered to be the principal offender. She was, within a few days after her arrival at Milton, summoned to appear for examination before MacLeod of Talisker, a captain of militia, in the Isle of Skye. Her friends importuned her to disobey the summons and secret herself amid the mountain fastnesses of their native isle. She peremptorily declined, declaring that she had done nothing of which she was ashamed, and would appear before any government official and answer any charges that might be instituted. Unprotected and alone she responded to the summons of Captain MacLeod, who permitted her to visit her mother at Armadale. Before reaching there she was seized by an officer in command of a party of soldiers and conveyed a prisoner on board the *Furnace,* commanded by Captain Ferguson. General John Campbell, happening to be on board the vessel, took her in charge and treated her with great consideration, permitting her to visit her mother, replenish her wardrobe, and to procure a female servant. On board this vessel she remained twenty-two days.

After many trials, much suffering, and several hairbreadth escapes, Prince Charles succeeded in eluding his pursuers, and on September 20 set sail from Loch Arkaig, on the mainland, on board the

Bellona of Nantes, and the twenty-ninth arrived at Roscort, near Morlaix, after narrowly escaping Admiral Lestock's squadron.

The narrative of the wanderings of the prince reads more like a romance than a reality, and is entertainingly set forth in various books, especially so in Keltie's *History of the Highland Clans,* Chamber's *History of the Rebellion of 1745-46,* and Boswell's *Tour of the Hebrides,* all of which contain full accounts of Flora MacDonald's participation in the prince's escape.

By order of General Campbell, Flora MacDonald was conveyed to Dunstaffnage Castle, where she was confined for about ten days. Here she received much attention, not only from the governor, but also from the most prominent families. From the castle she was taken and placed in a wherry, and before a stiff breeze the frail craft glided swiftly down Loch Etive towards the Sound of Mull, and soon disappeared. She was then put on board the *Bridgewater,* which put into Leith Roads early in September and remained there until November.

By this time the name of Flora MacDonald had become famous, and wherever the winds had wafted her deeds she was regarded as a heroine and greatly admired. While the *Bridgewater* was lying in Leith Roads she was almost constantly visited by the better class, both at Leith' and Edinburgh. All appeared to be interested in her and did what was in their power to add to her comfort. Her wise conduct, good sense, and fortitude impressed all alike.

The *Bridgewater,* in which Flora MacDonald was held a prisoner, left Leith Roads on November 7 and carried her direct to London. Her fame had preceded her to the metropolis and had excited as much interest as was exhibited in Scotland. The government, realizing that the nation deeply sympathized with the fair prisoner, deemed it would be unwise to commit her to the common gaol, and that it would injure their popularity if she was visited with the severity of the law, after a short confinement in the Tower, turned her over to the custody of friends who became responsible for her appearance when demanded. For nearly twelve months she remained a state prisoner. On the passage of the Indemnity Act, in July, 1747, Flora MacDonald was set at liberty. On receiving her liberation she became a guest of honor in the house of Lady Primrose, and was there visited by crowds of

Flora mcdonald

(From Original Painting by I. Mackluin, 1747)

the fashionable world who paid her great homage. Artists waited upon her to procure her portrait, and others to award their gifts. In London a subscription was raised for her amounting to £1,500. All this demonstration produced no effect on her mind but that of surprise; she had only performed an act of humanity, and never thought of it in any other light until she found the world making so much ado over it.

Before leaving London she particularly interested herself in the liberation of old Kingsburgh, a state prisoner in Scotland, and others, and was gratified at her success. When all matters were finally arranged, with her faithful Niel MacDonald she left London in a coach and four for Edinburgh. Leaving Edinburgh she proceeded to Inverness and became a guest among her friends for ten days. Thence, on horseback she journeyed to her mother's home at Armadale.

For two months she rested at her mother's home, and then visited her friends at Scalpa, Raasay, Scorribreck, Kingsburgh, Flodigarry, and especially at Monkstadt where Sir Alexander MacDonald and Lady Margaret rejoiced at her appearance. While staying at Scorribreck, Mr. Nicholson invited a large party of the neighboring ladies and gentlemen to meet the distinguished heroine. Among them was Major Allan MacDonald, who had, by a cunning device, arrested Flora's friend, Donald MacLeod of Galtrigal, and was the cause of his imprisonment. The major held out his hand to welcome Flora, whereupon she tartly said: "Yes, sir, I give you my hand, but not entirely with my heart. I wish to show all courtesy to the profession which you have disgraced by a low and base strategem utterly unworthy of the conduct of a soldier, a Highlander, and a gentleman!" This honest expression for a moment paralyzed the whole company.

A few visits were made among the respectable families in the vicinity of Portree, where all were delighted to receive her. Next she resorted to the mansion house of Kingsburgh, which was simply a heath-thatched cottage surrounded by trees. At that period there were but three slated houses on the island, not including Armadale, Dunvegan Castle, and a prison. The thatched houses were warm, comfortable, and well furnished. Unfortunately, Alexander MacDonald, who had recently returned from his long imprisonment in Edinburgh Castle, had gone to Flodigarry, in the north end of the island. From

Kingsburgh she repaired to Monkstadt, and during her stay the house was frequented by a great many visitors. It was on this occasion that Lady Margaret made the arrangements for Flora's marriage with Allen MacDonald, Kingsburgh's son.

BARBAQUE CREEK KIRK
(From MacLean's "Scotch Highlanders in America")

CHAPTER IV.

Marriage and Person.

It has been noted that Flora MacDonald had become famous at home as well as abroad. On her return to Uist she made her home with her brother at Milton. She made frequent visits to Lady Clanranald at Ormiclade, and other families in the Long Island, and on several occasions crossed to the Isle of Skye to visit in the family at Monkstadt, and to pass lengthened intervals with her mother at Armadale. It is also in evidence that during the latter part of the year 1748 she made a visit to London.

Early in life Flora formed an attachment to Allen, son of Alexander MacDonald of Kingsburgh. The marriage took place at Flodigarry, November 6, 1750, the festivities of which were on a large scale and lasted nearly a week, the company being unusually large. The bride was robed in a dress of the Stuart pattern, with which she had been presented by a lady friend when in London. An immense barn had been fitted up for the gentlemen's sleeping berths, and a similar place for ladies, while a pavilion was erected, and roofed with heather, to serve both for a banqueting hall and ball-room.

Flodigarry is situated in the north end of Skye, sixteen miles distant from Kingsburgh, and at that time was rented by Allen. It is one of the most romantic spots on the Isle, and of rare beauty. Here Flora and her husband remained until the death of old Kingsburgh, which took place February 13, 1772, aged 83.

Alexander MacDonald, Sixth of Kingsburgh, was a man of great integrity, probity, and honor, and was long one of the principal managers of his chief's affairs, having been first appointed by Sir Donald in 1718, and in his duties acquitted himself with great fidelity. In 1746 he assisted Prince Charles to escape, and for one night entertained him in his house. For this he was ordered arrested by the Duke of Cumberland and thrown into Edinburgh Castle. The arrest was made by General John Campbell, who sent him on parole, without any guard, to Fort Augustus, where he was plundered of everything, thrown into a dungeon and loaded with irons. Here he was examined by Sir Edward Fawkener, who reminded him of the noble opportunity he had lost by not betraying the prince. To this Kingsburgh righteously replied, "Had I gold and silver piled heaps upon heaps to the bulk of yon huge mountain, that mass could not afford me half the satisfaction I find in my own heart from doing what I have done." Another officer came and asked him if he would know the young pretender's head if he saw it. He replied that he would know it very well if he saw it on his shoulders. "But if the head were not on the shoulders, do you think you should know it in that case?" "In that case," answered Kingsburgh, "I will not pretend to know anything about it." He was removed to Edinburgh Castle under a strong guard, and there placed in a room by himself, which he was not allowed to leave, nor see any one except those in charge. Here he was kept until liberated, July 4, 1747; having, as one author observed, "got a whole year's lodging for affording that of one night."

Kingsburgh sustained heavy losses in consequence of the part he took in the prince's cause, and to his personal removal from the management of his affairs by a year's imprisonment in Edinburgh Castle. Added to this he was deprived of the remunerative management of his chief's extensive estates.

Allen MacDonald was one of the most handsome and powerful members of his clan, and possessed superior qualities of both mind and body. Boswell, in his *Tour of the Hebrides,* who first saw him on September 12, 1773, thus describes him: "Kingsburgh was completely the figure of a gallant Highlander, exhibiting the graceful mien and manly looks, which our popular Scotch song has justly attributed to that character. He had his tartan plaid thrown about him, a large blue bonnet with a knot of black ribband like a cockade, a brown short coat of a kind of duffil, a tartan waistcoat with gold buttons and gold button-holes, a bluish philibeg, and tartan hose. He had jet black hair tied behind, and was a large, stately man, with a steady, sensible countenance."

Boswell and Dr. Samuel Johnson made it a point to visit Kingsburgh House during their tour of the Hebrides, being attracted by the fame of its mistress. Boswell speaks of her as "a little woman, of a genteel appearance, and uncommonly mild and well-bred."

Doctor Johnson, through the kindness of Flora, was permitted to sleep in the bed occupied by Prince Charles, and also to use the same sheets, which greatly pleased him. In his *Journey to the Western Isles* he was moved to say: "We were entertained with the usual hospitality by Mr. MacDonald and his lady, Flora MacDonald, a name that will be mentioned in history, and if courage and fidelity be virtues, mentioned with honor. She is a woman of middle stature, soft features, gentle manners, and elegant presence." In the morning on which he left Kingsburgh, a slip of paper was found on his toilet table, with the following Latin words written in pencil: "Quantum cedat virtutibus aurum," which Doctor Carruthers, in his *Notes to Boswell's Tour*, freely translates, "With virtue sacrificed, what worthless trash is gold."

While imprisoned on board the *Bridgewater*, in Leith Roads, Flora was visited by Bishop Forbes, who thus describes her: "Although she was easy and cheerful, yet she had a certain mixture of gravity in all her behaviour which became her situation exceedingly well, and set her off to great advantage. She is of a low stature, of a fair complexion, and well enough shaped. One would not discern by her conversation that she had spent all her former days in the Highlands; for she talks English (or rather Scots) easily, and not at all through the Erse tone. She has a sweet voice, and sings well, and no lady, Edinburgh-bred, can acquit herself better at the tea-table than she did when in Leith Roads. Her wise conduct in one of the most perplexing scenes that can happen in life, her fortitude and good sense are memorable instances of the strength of a female mind, even in those years that are tender and inexperienced."

In North Carolina it is a tradition, handed down by those who knew her, that she was "a dignified and handsome woman, to whom all paid great respect." It is the united testimony that at the time she left for America she still retained much of the beauty of her youth.

Thomas Pennant visited Kingsburgh July 22, and 23, 1772. The only reference to the heroine he makes is the following paragraph:

FLORA MACDONALD MEETING DOCTOR JOHNSON
(From "Boswell's "Tour to the Hebrides")

"After a passage of a mile landed at Kingsburgh, immortalized by its mistress, the celebrated Flora MacDonald, the fair protectress of a fugitive adventurer, who, after some days concealing himself from pursuit, in the disguise of the lady's maid, here flung off the female habit." However he remarks he was "lodged this night in the same bed that formerly received the unfortunate Charles Stuart," besides commenting on three very curious, ancient relics given him by Allen. In Pinkerton's *General Collection of Voyages and Travels,* I find this sentence inserted in the text: "I had the pleasure of her acquaintance at the first Sir Watkin William Wynne's in the year 1746; but at this time I unfortunately found that she was absent on a visit."

CHAPTER V.

Financial Embarrassment of Allen MacDonald.

It must have been a matter of common notoriety that Allen Mac-Donald was greatly embarrassed financially. Boswell speaks of it as no secret, and refers to it in the following language: "In reality my heart was grieved, when I recollected that Kingsburgh was embarrassed in his affairs, and intended to go to America." This arose from no mismanagement or extravagance of his own or that of his prudent wife, but from the heavy losses of his father, growing out of the troublous times and the part he took in it. The losses appear to have been very great. As the representative of his father, Allen became entangled, but in the face of all his endeavors to surmount the liabilities he found his efforts would prove futile.

The estate, known as Kingsburgh, was a part of the domain of Sir Alexander MacDonald of the Isles, and was occupied by the chamberlain. The first Kingsburgh was James MacDonald, brother of Donald Gorm MacDonald of Sleat, Lord of the Isles, who lived during the times of James V. and Queen Mary. He was succeeded by his son, John, who was killed at the battle of Lichd Li, fought by nearly the whole clan against the MacLeans of Mull. Allen was the seventh and last of Kingsburgh.

The removal to America was deliberately considered by Allen and Flora, and the conclusion was probably arrived at by the spirit of emigration that had seized the MacDonalds.

CHAPTER VI.

Flora MacDonald Removes to America.

America had long sought emigrants from Europe, and some of the governors of the provinces interested themselves in arranging for such settlers as were seeking new homes. North Carolina had been a tempting field. The region of the Cape Fear River presented peculiar attractions. It was a beautiful country, the climate mild, there were the tall pines on the uplands, the bottoms covered with rich canebrakes, an abundance of small game, and a soil adapted to the general wants. When the Highlanders first noticed the country there is no documentary evidence, but it is positively known that there was a settlement at the head of navigation of the Cape Fear as early as 1729. There is a tradition that many Highlanders had located on the river immediately after the disastrous rising in 1715. At the time of the arrival of Flora MacDonald the Highland settlements had spread beyond the Cape Fear, and as high up as the confluence of the Deep and Haw, and to the Pedee where the Yadkin and Uwharie came together, and embraced the present counties of Cumberland, Harnett, Moore, Montgomery, Anson, Richmond, Robeson, and Scotland, and even entering beyond the State line into South Carolina.

The greatest migration was that immediately following the battle of Culloden, in 1746, led by Neill McNeill, of Jura, the people having been driven from their homes by oppression. These emigrants were of the very best types, well formed, strong, enterprising, and deeply religious. Previous to this time, in 1739, Neill had brought, principally from Argyleshire, three hundred and fifty, and settled them on the Cape Fear. Great numbers of families, during the years 1746 and 1747, came to North Carolina, and settled about Cross Creek (now Fayetteville) in Cumberland County. There was a North Carolina mania for emigration which pervaded all classes, from the poorest crofter to the well-to-do farmer, and men of easy competence, who

VIEW FROM BEINN, NA, CAILLICH IN SKYE,
(From Pennant's "Tour in Scotland." Taken in 1772)

were, according to an appropriate song of the day, "Dol a dh'iarruidh an fhortain do North Carolina."

The emigration to America from the Highlands of Scotland was so pronounced that the Scottish papers made frequent reference to it and bemoaned the prevalence. The *Scots Magazine* for September, 1769, records that the ship *Molly* sailed from Islay on August 21, full of passengers for North Carolina, which was the third emigration from Argyle "since the close of the late war." A subsequent issue of the same paper states that fifty-four vessels full of emigrants from the Western Islands and other parts of the Highlands sailed for North Carolina between April and July, 1770, conveying twelve hundred emigrants. Early in 1771, the same magazine states that five hundred emigrants in Islay and adjoining isles were preparing to sail for America. Again it records that the ship *Adventure* sailed from Loch Erribol, Sunday, August 17, 1772, with upwards of two hundred emigrants from Sutherlandshire for North Carolina. Other reports might be referred to. In 1772 the great MacDonald emigration commenced, and continued until the outbreak of the American Revolution. It was during this period that the MacDonalds outnumbered any of the other clans in North America. The Revolution stopped emigration, which did not break out again until 1805.

The emigrants maintained their manners, customs, language, and religion, all of which have now changed, except their religion, which has been modified. A person passing through the North Carolina country inhabited by the Scotch Highlanders would have seen many a warrior who had fought at Preston, at Falkirk, and at Culloden. He was still the plaided warrior, though his claymore was sheathed.

The MacDonald emigration swept Allen and Flora MacDonald into its current. Flora was ready and willing to sacrifice everything for her husband's comfort, and to accompany him to any quarter where he might surmount his difficulties. In making their domestic arrangements, the son, John, was placed under the care of Sir Alexander Mac-Kenzie of Delvin, until he was of age, for an India appointment, and a girl, then nine years of age, was left with friends. The other children accompanied their parents, who set sail on board the *Baliol* from

Campbelton, Kintyre, for North Carolina, in the month of August,
1774. They left the

"Land of grey rock and drifting rain,
Of clamorous brook and boisterous main,—
Of treacherous squall and furious gale,
That bend the mast or rend the sail—,
Land of green pine and harebell blue,
Of furze and fern of various hue;
Of deep ravine, and cavern hoar;
Of jutting crag and dangerous shore.

"Land of the pibroch and the plaid;
Land of the henchman and the raid;
Land of the chieftain and the clan,
Of haughty laird and vassal-man,
Of Kelt, of Gael, of Catheran.
Land of tall cliff and lonely dell,
The eagle's perch, the outlaw's cell;—
Land of the brave, the fair, the good;
Land of the onslaught, foray, feud;
Land of the ptarmigan and roe;
Land where Glenlivat's fountains flow,
Sparkling and bright as 'mountain dew,'
The heart to warm, the strength renew.
Land of the long, long wintry night,
The dancing, streaming boreal light;
The misty morn, the brightening noon,
The dewy eve, the radiant moon;
Land of the sprightly reel and glee;
The wraith, the fairy, the banshee;
Land where the patriot loves to roam
Far distant from his native home;
And yet, on every foreign strand,
Still sighing for his native land!

"Land of basaltic rock and cave,
Where tempests howl and surges rave;
Where Fingal sat and Ossian sung,
While Staffa's echoing caverns rung
With feats achiev'd by heroes' arms,
With tragic tales and war's alarms,
With lover's vows and lady's charms.

"Land of the heathery hill and moor,
Of rude stone cot and cold clay floor;
Of barefoot nymph and tartan'd boor.

"Land of the kirk, austere and pure,
From pope and prelacy secure,—
With pastor grave and flock demure.
Land of the metaphysic strife,
Where mortal's lot in future life
Is settled by presumptuous man,
Who dares the Almighty's ways to scan!

WOMEN AT THE QUERN AND FULLING CLOTH, WITH A VIEW OF TALISKER

(From Pennant's "Tour of Scotland." Taken in 1772)

"Land of the eagle's airy nest,
On Glencoe's cliffs or Nevis' crest;
Land of the lochs, that winding sweep
Round mountain's base and headland steep.
Land of the tottering keep and tower,
O'er moat that frown, o'er surge that lower;—
Land of the thousand isles that sleep
'Twixt lowering cloud and murmuring deep;
Land of the thousand barks that ride
O'er curling wave or confluent tide;
And, without aid of oar or sail,
Urge their fleet course 'gainst tide or gale.

     *   *   *   *   *   *   *   *

"Land where the torrents leap from high,
And o'er their rocky barriers fly
In sheets of foam, with thundering roar,
Down through the dark ravine to pour;
          the signal gives to weigh;
The wi. . . .rd tides brook no delay.
Bleak Mull, farewell! I must away."

What were the thoughts of Flora MacDonald as she caught the last glimpse of Skye, or how deep was the poetic part of her nature, we will never know. It may be she thought the sentiment, if not the language of the poet:

"Farewell, lovely Skye, sweet isle of my childhood,
    Thy blue mountains I'll clamber no more;
Thy heath-skirted corries, green valleys and wildwood,
    I now leave behind for a far-distant shore.
Adieu, ye stern cliffs, clad in old, hoary grandeur;
    Adieu, ye still dingles, fond haunts of the roe.

"How painful to part from the misty-robed Coollin,
    The Alps of Great Britain, with antlered peaks high;
Bold Glamaig, Coruisk, and sublime Scuirnagillin,
    Make mainland grand mountains look dull, tame, and shy.
Majestic Quiraing, fairy place of Nature,
    Stormy Idrigill, Hailleaval, and cloud-piercing Stoer,
And the shining Spar-cave, like some beacon to heaven,
    All I deeply lament, and may never see more!

"Once more, dearest isle, let me gaze on thy mountains,
    Once more let the village church gleam on my view;
And my ear drink the music of murmuring fountains,
    While I bid to my old and my young friends adieu.
Farewell, lovely Skye, lake, mountain, and corrie;
    Brown isle of the valiant, the brave, and the free;
Ever green to thy sod, resting-place of my Flora,
    My sighs are for Skye, my tears are for thee."

The good ship *Baliol* had a very favorable passage to the Western World. The time of the departure of Flora MacDonald was known to her kindred and countrymen in North Carolina, where she was anxiously expected and joyfully received on her arrival. Her name was as well known among them as it was in Scotland, and held in just as great esteem. Many had known her in childhood and early womanhood, though some had not seen her since the rising of 1745. All these people, and others, felt proud of the prospect that she should cross the ocean to become one of their number. A royal welcome was determined upon, which was actuated by a genuine feeling of love, admiration, and praise for her heroism and noble character. Demonstrations, on a large scale, were made to welcome her to America, and her new home, wherever she might decide to become a denizen. Soon after her landing a largely-attended ball was given in her honor at Wilmington, when she was greatly gratified by the special attention bestowed on her daughter, Anne, then entering into womanhood, and of surpassing beauty.

From Wilmington the Kingsburgh family proceeded to Cross Creek, then regarded as the capital of the Highland settlement. Before reaching Cross Creek the party was met by a large procession in order that Flora might be properly escorted into their midst. As she approached the capital, the strains of the *Piobaireachd,* and the martial airs of her native land fell upon the ears of the multitude. In the vast concourse of people were some of her old neighbors and kinsfolks, many of whom had crossed the Atlantic years before. Their faces, manner, and voices bore testimony to the welcome of the heart. Many families of distinction pressed upon her to make their dwellings her home, but she respectfully declined, preferring a settled abode of her own.

As the Laird of Kingsburgh had decided to become a planter, he left his family in Cross Creek until he had secured a permanent location. The house in which the family is said to have lived during this period was built immediately upon the brink of the creek, and for many years after was known as "Flora MacDonald's house," although during my brief visit there four different spots were pointed out as being the site of her residence. It is possible that the various places are remembered from the fact that she was there entertained. During her stay she visited and received visits from her friends, one of whom was Mrs. Rutherford, afterwards Mrs. McAuslin, who, at that time, lived in a house known as the "Stuart Place," north of the Presbyterian Church. Here she saw a painting which represented "Anne of Jura," assisting the prince to escape. "Turn the face of that picture to the wa'," she said. "Never let it see the light again. It belies the truth of history. Anne of Jura was na' there, and did na' help the bonnie prince."

A large number of MacDonalds, principally from Skye and Raasay, and kinsmen of Kingsburgh, had settled northwest of Cross Creek, a distance of twenty miles, about a hill some six hundred feet in height, now called Cameron's Hill, but then known as Mount Pleasant. Here Kingsburgh purchased a large tract of land, the record of the deed is still preserved in the court-house at Fayetteville. Hard by are the sources of Barbaque Creek, and not many miles down the stream stood the old kirk, where the clansmen worshipped, and where Flora inscribed her name on the roll of membership. This church, with that called Longstreet (where Flora also at times worshipped) appears to have been founded in 1758 by Rev. James Campbell, a native of Campbelton, Argyleshire, Scotland. But at the time of Flora's arrival the churches were served by Rev. John McLeod.

Having been persuaded by Colonel MacQueen, Allen disposed of his estate and removed farther west, and, in January, 1776, purchased of Caleb Touchstone a tract of land numbering 550 acres, then in Anson County, but now forming a part of Richmond. The plantation is located eighteen miles north of Rockingham, two miles north of Capel's Mills, on Mountain Creek, and about five miles north of Ellerbe Springs. Allen named the estate Killiegrey, which contained a dwelling and out-houses, which were more pretentious than was then customary among Highland settlers. The outlay cost him four hundred and sixty pounds. The new home was situated in the heart of the pinery region, and in every direction the great pine forest stretched forth. Here the Kingsburgh family immediately established itself, and Flora felt assured that with her family she would spend her remaining days in peace and happiness. Flora and Allen, her husband, were the most commanding figures among all the Highlanders in North Carolina. Their influence was everywhere felt and acknowledged. The power for good was placed in their hands, and wisdom would have suggested that in wielding it a conservative policy should be pursued.

CHAPTER VII.

RISING OF THE HIGHLANDERS IN 1776.

The dreams of Flora MacDonald of peace, happiness, and prosperity were doomed to a rude awakening. Before she was well settled in her new home the storm of the American Revolution burst upon her in all its fury. That she was partially responsible for the final disaster that accomplished the complete financial ruin of the family is beyond question; for she was an active participant in arousing the Highlanders to resistance. Without any hesitation she used her powerful influence in forcing the insurrection of 1776. Notwithstanding this, the disaster would not have overtaken the family had Kingsburgh refrained from precipitating himself into the conflict needlessly and recklessly. His age and past experience should have influenced his course, and bade him remain a silent spectator of the conflict. With blind fatuity he took the wrong side in the struggle, and even then, by the exercise of patience he might have overcome the effects of his folly.

The British authorities bent on the subjugation of the Thirteen Colonies, looked to the formidable Highland Scotch settlements along the Cape Fear and the Mohawk for assistance. The frightful atrocities following the disaster on Drummossie Muir, and the relentless persecution of the Highland clans did not wean that hardy race from the merciless hand of the victor. The American Revolution found all Scotland its pitiless foe. Petition after petition went up from city, town, and hamlet to George III., expressing intense feelings against the Americans, and all protesting that the respective petitioners were the most loyal subjects. Over seven thousand Highlanders, born in Scotland, fought against Washington and his compatriots.

The records demonstrate that the emigrants from the Highlands were received with open arms by the colonists and rendered every assistance needed. Some of the emigrants were destitute even of the means of procuring assistance. Even after the call to armed resistance had been obeyed, a shipload of Highlanders was stranded in Virginia, and every care was rendered by the colonists.

On the breaking out of hostilities, the Highlanders became an object of consideration to the contending parties. They were numerically strong, increasing in numbers, and their military qualities second to none. British emissaries were sent among all of them, though it was known that their inclination strongly favored the royal cause, and that side left no means untried to cement their loyalty, even to appeals to their religious natures. To counteract the efforts of the royalists the Americans were at a great disadvantage, because it was impossible for them to secure a Gaelic-speaking minister, clothed with authority to go among them. Even the resources and loyalty of Rev. James Campbell would be counteracted by Rev. John McLeod, because he stood nearer to the MacDonalds and MacLeods, the two dominant clans. His sympathies were thrown against the Americans, and his actions were of such a nature that it was deemed prudent to arrest him, but he was discharged on May 11, 1776.

No steps were taken by the Americans to enroll the Highlanders into military companies. Their efforts were made to enlist the sympathies of the clansmen. On the other hand, the royal governor, Josiah Martin, took steps to enroll the North Carolina settlers into active British service. The governor was in constant communication with them, and, in a measure, directed their movements. Allen MacDonald of Kingsburgh was the recognized leader. As early as July 3, 1775, he went to Fort Johnson, and there concerted with Governor Martin regarding the raising of a battalion of "good and faithful Highlanders," fully calculating on the recently-settled MacDonalds and MacLeods. Prior communications were held between Martin and Kingsburgh, because the former recommended that the latter should be appointed major, in his communication to Lord Dartmouth, on June 30 preceding. In the report of the same to the same, dated November 12, 1775, the statement is made that Kingsburgh had raised a company, as had also his son-in-law, Alexander MacLeod. From the official records, it may therefore be seen that the Laird of Kingsburgh was not drawn into the controversy under restraint or under solicitation. How far his early steps in the matter were influenced by his wife, Flora, will never be known; but, in all probability, he took no action without her knowledge and consent. Whatever view we may take of their action, whether it be censure or praise, it must be admitted that both were governed by their sense of right and justice. It is but fair in judging the motives of every one to put ourselves exactly in the position of the one adjudged. The sense of right, *per se,* is an entirely different thing.

It is not to be presumed that the Provincial Congress of North Carolina, and other patriotic bodies, were not aroused in every particular. We find that the Congress, on August 23, 1775, appointed from among its members Archibald MacLaine, Alexander McAllister, Farquhard Campbell, Alexander McKay, and others, "a committee to confer with the gentlemen who have lately arrived from the Highlands in Scotland to settle in this province, and to explain to them the nature of our unhappy controversy with Great Britain, and to advise and urge them to unite with the other inhabitants of America in defense of their rights which they derive from God and the Constitution."

Governor Martin stood ready to precipitate matters and involve the Highlanders in a quarrel with the other inhabitants; for in his letter to Lord Dartmouth, of June 30, 1775, he declares he "could collect immediately among the emigrants from the Highlands of Scotland," "three thousand effective men," and begs permission "to raise a battalion of a thousand Highlanders here," and "I would most humbly beg leave to recommend Mr. Allen MacDonald of Kingsburgh to be major, and Captain Alexd. McLeod of the marines now on half-pay to be first captain, who, besides being men of great worth and good character, have most extensive influence over the Highlanders here, a great part of which are of their own names and families."

On November 12, following, the governor again writes that he can "assure your lordship that the Scotch Highlanders here are generally and almost without exception staunch to government," and that Captain Alexander McLeod, a gentleman from the Highlands of Scotland and late an officer in the marines, who has been settled in this province about a year and is one of the gentlemen I had the honor to recommend to your lordship to be appointed a captain in the battalion of Highlanders, I proposed with his Majesty's permission to raise here, found his way down to me at this place about three weeks ago, and I learn from him that he is, as well as his father-in-law, Mr. Allen Mac-Donald, proposed to me for major of the intended corps, moved by my encouragements have each raised a company of Highlanders since which a Major McDonald who came here some time ago from Boston under the orders from General Gage to raise Highlanders to form a battalion* to be commanded by Lieut. Coll. Allan McLean, has made them proposals of being appointed captains in that corps, which they have accepted on the condition that his Majesty does not approve my proposal of raising a battalion of Highlanders and reserving to themselves the choice of appointments therein in case it shall meet with his Majesty's approbation in support of that measure."

The activities of the royalists during the year 1775 were so pronounced as to cause the patriots to be on the alert. For some reason the Highlanders were visited by General Lachlan McIntosh of the Georgia Highlanders, who was born in Badenoch, Scotland, in 1725, but had been in America since the age of eleven. He used every argument in his power to induce his countrymen in North Carolina to remain neutral in the conflict then impending, as it was the only safe and consistent course for them to take. In answer, the agents of Governor Martin appealed to their professions of loyalty, their love of their native country, that all efforts against the king had proved abortive, and that all who resisted the government would be dealt with as were their fathers and brothers after the battle of Culloden, besides reminding them of their oath of allegiance.

Against these delusive arguments General McIntosh reminded them that they had no attachment for the reigning house of Hanover, and there was no inducement to risk anything in maintaining its authority; that they had already suffered severely, on several occasions, by the arbitrary and unjust measures of the present government, and that they need expect nothing better in times to come. He further assured them that if they would remain quietly at home, he had no doubts that he would succeed in procuring their safety and peace. The appeals of McIntosh were so forcible that all consented save a few military characters, some hot-headed young men, and a majority of

---

*For an account of this regiment see MacLean's Scotch Highlanders in America, Chapter XIII.

Clans MacDonald and MacLeod. Unfortunately, directly after his departure the arrival of Donald McDonald and Donald McLeod, assisted by the Laird of Kingsburgh, overturned the good that had been reached. McDonald was sixty-five years of age, had fought at Culloden and Bunker Hill, and was sent, with McLeod, from Boston, by General Gage, to take command of the Highlanders in North Carolina. They came by way of Newbern, where they were arrested, but pretended that they were wounded at Bunker Hill, and had left the army with the design of settling among their friends. They arrived in June, 1775, and immediately set out on their mission.

The Laird of Kingsburgh early came under the suspicion of the Committee of Safety at Wilmington. On the very day, July 3, 1775, he was in consultation with Governor Martin, its chairman was directed to write to him "to know from himself respecting the reports that circulate of his having an intention to raise troops to support the arbitrary measures of the ministry against the Americans in this colony, and whether he had not made an offer of his services to Governor Martin for that purpose:"

On August 21, 1775, the Provincial Congress began its session at Hillsboro. Cumberland County was represented by Farquhard Campbell, Thomas Rutherford, Alexander McKay, Alexander McAlister, and Daniel Smith. Campbellton sent Joseph Hepburn. Among the members of this Congress having distinctly Highland names, besides those already mentioned, were John Campbell and John Johnston from Bertie, Samuel Johnston of Chowan, Duncan Lamon of Edgecombe, John McNitt Alexander of Mecklenburg, Kenneth McKenzie of Martin, Jeremiah Frazier of Tyrell, William Graham of Tryon, and Archibald Maclaine of Wilmington. One of the acts of this Congress was to divide the State into military districts and the appointment of field officers of the Minute Men. For Cumberland County, Thomas Rutherford was appointed colonel; Alexander McAllister, lieutenant-colonel; Duncan McNeill, first major; Alexander McDonald, second major. One company of Minute Men was to be raised. The act was passed on September 9.

How many proved unfaithful to the interests at first avowed, I am unable to determine. Prominent among those who proved recreant to their trust we find the names of Thomas Rutherford and Farquhard Campbell. The latter dealt treacherously with both sides.

During the year 1775 no overt acts were committed, although in the northern provinces the contest had become bloody, and the Continental Congress had an army besieging Boston. True, military companies had been formed by both contestants, and as late as November and December, 1775, the two parties in Cross Creek mustered on opposite sides of the village, then returned into town and lived in great harmony.

On the Cape Fear were intelligent, public-spirited, and patriotic men who were determined to resist all encroachments, and who became very active in impressing upon the people of their respective neighborhoods the duty and importance of maintaining their liberties and resisting the oppression of the English government. Among these the most noted were Colonels James Moore, John Ashe, Alexander Lillington, Robert Rowan, and Thomas Robeson.

The early intrigues by the British agents with the Scotch Highlanders were more guessed at than known by the patriots. The early days of 1776 saw the masque torn from the face, and the intrigues reached their culmination. The war party among the Highlanders was greatly in the ascendant. The Americans, while at first they felt anxious, now had their feelings changed to bitterness, owing to the fact that they were not only precipitating themselves into a quarrel in which they had no special cause, but also were exhibiting ingratitude to those who had been their benefactors. Up to this time the Americans had only sought a redress of grievances, and but very few foresaw the ultimate outcome. True, the Highlanders had viewed the matter from a different standpoint. They failed to realize the craftiness of Governor Martin in compelling all who had recently arrived to take the oath of allegiance, which, with all the sacredness of religion, they felt to be binding. They had ever been taught that all promises were sacred, and a liar was a greater criminal than a thief. Still, it must be granted, they had every opportunity to learn the true status of the situation; independence had not yet been proclaimed; Washington was still in his trenches about Boston, and the Americans continued to petition the British throne to take cognizance of their grievances.

What the Highlanders expected to gain by their proposed actions would be difficult even to conjecture. They certainly failed to realize the condition of the country, and the insuperable difficulties to be overcome before they could make a junction with Sir Henry Clinton. Even should they assemble peaceably in Wilmington, there they would be one hundred miles from their homes and families, who would necessarily be at the mercy of their enemies, who had become bitter on account of their own actions. They were blinded and exhibited a want of ordinary foresight. There was also an exhibition of reckless indifference of the responsible parties to the welfare of those they had so successfully duped. During all the years which have elapsed since their ill-advised action, though treated with the utmost charity, their bravery applauded, even by their descendants they have been condemned for their rude precipitancy, besides failing to realize the changed condition of affairs, and not resenting the injuries they had received from the House of Hanover that had harried their country and hanged their fathers on the murderous gallows-tree.

Lieutenant Alexander McLean and Donald McLeod had been the trusted agents of Governor Martin to the back counties of North Carolina. They had returned with flattering reports, which he was not slow in transmitting to Sir Henry Clinton. Based partly on these reports, a vigorous campaign was determined on for 1776, the brunt of which was to fall upon North Carolina. The program was for Sir Henry Clinton, with a fleet of ships and seven corps of Irish regulars, to be at the mouth of the Cape Fear early in the year 1776, and there form a junction with the Highlanders and others to be raised from the interior. Believing that this armament would arrive in January or early in February, Martin made preparations for the revolt; for his "unwearied, persevering agent," Alexander McLean, brought written assurances from the principal persons to whom he had been directed, that between two and three thousand men would take the field at the governor's summons. Under this encouragement McLean was again sent into the back country with a commission dated January 10, 1776, authorizing Allen MacDonald, Donald MacDonald, Alexander McLeod, Donald McLeod, Alexander McLean, Allen Stewart, William Campbell, Alexander McDonald, and Neal McArthur, of Cumberland and

Anson counties, besides seventeen other persons, not connected with the Highlanders, who resided in a belt of counties in middle Carolina, to raise and array all the king's loyal subjects, and to march them in a body to Brunswick by February 15.

It has been argued because Allen MacDonald of Kingsburgh's name appears first in the list, it was designed by Governor Martin that he should be first in command. This conclusion is not warranted by the facts. Donald MacDonald was sent direct from Boston in order to take military command of the troops, and for several months had been on the ground. He came with the commission of major, and Martin had no authority to issue a higher commission. Besides this, the commission of Donald antedates that of Allen. Martin did commission Donald brigadier-general, but this was unauthorized. Said commission is still in Fayetteville. If Allen had any experience as a military commander the fact has not been recorded in history. He was in hiding for a while after the battle of Culloden, but this was on account of the arrest of old Kingsburgh, his father.

Upon receiving his orders from Governor Martin, at once General MacDonald issued the following:

By His Excellency Brigadier-General Donald McDonald, Commander of His Majesty's Forces for the time being in North Carolina:

"A MANIFESTO.

WHEREAS, I have received information that many of His Majesty's faithful subjects have been so far overcome by apprehension of danger as to fly before His Majesty's Army as from the most inveterate enemy; to remove which, as far as lies in my power, I have thought it proper to publish this Manifesto, declaring that I shall take the proper steps to prevent any injury being done, either to the person or properties of His Majesty's subjects; and I do further declare it to be my determined resolution, that no violence shall be used to women and children, as viewing such outrages to be inconsistent with humanity, and as tending in their consequences to sully the arms of Britons and soldiers.

I, therefore, in His Majesty's name, generally invite every well-wisher to that form of government under which they have so happily lived, and which, if justly considered, ought to be esteemed the best birthright of Britons and Americans, to repair to His Majesty's Royal Standard, erected at Cross Creek, where they will meet with every possible civility, and be ranked in the list of friends and fellow-soldiers, engaged in the best and most glorious of all causes, supporting the rights and constitution of their country. Those, therefore, who have been under the unhappy necessity of submitting to the mandates of Congress and committees—those lawless, usurped, and arbitrary tribunals— will have an opportunity (by joining the King's Army), to restore peace and tranquility to this distracted land—to open again the glorious streams of commerce—to partake of the blessings of inseparable from a regular administration of justice, and be again reinstated in the favorable opinion of their Sovereign.

DONALD MCDONALD.

By His Excellency's command.

KENN MCDONALD, P.S.

On February 5, after a conference with the principal leaders, General MacDonald issued another manifesto in which he declares it to be his "intention that no violation whatever shall be offered to women, children, or private property to sully the arms of Britons or freemen employed in the glorious and righteous cause of rescuing and delivering this country from the usurpation of rebellion, and that no cruelty whatever be offered against the laws of humanity, but what resistance shall make necessary; and that whatever provisions and other necessaries be taken for the troops shall be paid for immediately; and in case any person, or persons, shall offer the least violence to the families of such as will join the Royal Standard, such person or persons may depend that retaliation will be made; the horror of such proceedings, it is hoped, will be avoided by all true Christians."

Manifestos being the order of the day, Thomas Rutherford, erstwhile patriot, deriving his commission from the Provincial Congress, though having alienated himself, but signing himself colonel, also issued one in which he declared that this is "to command, enjoin, beseech, and require all His Majesty's faithful subjects within the County of Cumberland to repair to the King's Royal Standard, at Cross Creek, on or before the sixteenth, present, in order to join the King's army; otherwise, they must expect to fall under the melancholy consequences of a declared rebellion, and expose themselves to the just resentment of an injured, though gracious Sovereign."

On February 1, General MacDonald erected the royal standard at

Cross Creek, in the public square, and in order to cause the Highlanders to respond with alacrity, various methods were employed that
the military spirit might be freely inculcated.

The call came like an emergency, summoning the disaffected to
the standard of the king. To many of the Highlanders it was a slogan,
a veritable firey cross hurled over the sand hills and the pine forests.
But there were others who still needed awakening and appeared to
realize that danger lurked in the distance. Those holding the minor
commissions in the military service found it necessary to become exceedingly active and to use every means and exertion in their power.
Efforts were not only made among the Highlanders, but also among
the Regulators, who generally sympathized with the British notwithstanding their terrible defeat at the battle of Alamance on May 16, 1771.
The rendezvous of the latter was at Cross Hill, less than two miles
from the present town of Carthage, where about five hundred assembled, some of whom, however, were Highlanders. Owing to the
fact that the Highland army moved out of Cross Creek before the
time appointed, Colonel William Fields failed to join the command.
He was on his way with his regiment, but learning of the defeat at
Moore's Creek, returned home.

At Cross Hill the military array was met by General MacDonald,
who formally erected the king's standard, and had the governor's proclamation read along with the military commissions which had been
given. An organization was made in due form, so far as was prac-
ticable, but the claims for office were too great to be satisfied.

The Scotch were an entirely different people from the Regulators.
From time immemorial they had been warlike. If not engaged in contending against a common enemy, they had their training in the conflict
of clan against clan. No land of the same territorial limits and the
same population abounds more in legendary, traditionary, and historical narratives of hard-fought battles, personal encounters, and perilous
adventures. Fortunately the accounts have been preserved by their
bards, a noted class even from the days of Ossian down to the present
hour. During the long nights of winter, in Scotland, the tales were
rehearsed in various huts where the people would assemble. Then,
again, the sound of the pibroch would at any time arouse the martial

spirit of the people, from the mere lad to the man of great age; for old and young were upon the field of carnage.

At the opening of the campaign of 1776, most of the Highlanders had reached the age of fifty or more, and had imbibed military spirit from infancy, cherished in youth, and exhibited the same in manhood. In America all the legends and tales were taught the youth, just the same as though they were living on the ancient clan lands of Scotland.

The sound of the pibroch was now heard in the pine forests of America summoning the clansmen to arms. Nightly balls were inaugurated that the people might assemble and be properly enthused. The war spirit of Flora MacDonald was stirred within her. Night after night she attended these gatherings; addressed the men in their native Gaelic, and urged them to enter the king's army. During the day, on horseback, with her husband, she went from house to house and used her persuasive powers to excite the slow, the indifferent, and doubtful to action. To her personal appeals the success of the gathering was largely due.

According to the *American Historical Review* of 1872, the following letter, written by Flora MacDonald, was preserved in Fayetteville in 1852:

FEBRUARY 1, 1776.

DEAR MAGGIE: Allan leaves tomorrow to join Donald's standard at Cross Creek, and I shall be alone wi' my three bairns. Canna ye come and stay wi' me awhile? There are troublous times ahead I ween. God will keep the right. I hope all our ain are in the right, prays your good friend,   FLORY McDONALD.

Other influences of a far different nature were at work. Caruthers, in his *Revolutionary Incidents,* gives an example, in the case of Hugh MacDonald, who declared that General MacDonald and Donald Mac-Leod persuaded the Scotch "to step forward and draw their broad swords, as their forefathers had often done, in defense of their king, who would give them double wages and double honors." "These gentlemen, notwithstanding their influence among the ignorant Scotch, were instigated by selfish and speculative motives; and not only they, but their subaltern officers also. I well recollect, though only entering on my fourteenth year, that John Martin, who called himself a captain in the contemplated regiment, came to the home of my father, who then lived near the place now known by the name of Carthage, in Moore County; and, after causing him to enlist, told him that he must take me along with him. My father said that I would be of no service in the army as a soldier, and as his wife was a sickly woman and the children all weakly, I would be useful at home to the family. *'Never mind your family,'* was his reply, *'he will count one to procure me a commission,* and he will draw you a soldier's pay.' My father told him that would be unjust. 'If you do not take him with you, I will see you hanged when we see the king,' was his reply to that; and my father was afraid of his threats, knowing that when offended he was not too strict in points of honor. Five days after this they were embodied and marched to Cross Creek."

At length the time arrived for the gathering at Cross Creek. Then the Highlanders were seen coming from near and from far, from the wide plantations on the river bottoms, and from the rude cabins in the depths of the lonely pine forests, with the claymore at their side, in tartan garments and feathered bonnet, and keeping step to the shrill music of the bag-pipe. There came, first of all, Clan MacDonald, with Clan MacLeod near at hand, with lesser numbers of Clan MacKenzie, Clan MacRae, Clan MacLean, Clan MacKay, Clan MacLachlan, and still others. There were also about two hundred Regulators. As may be inferred, all who were capable of bearing arms did not respond, because some would not engage in a cause where their traditions and affections had no part, some of whom hid in the swamps and others in the forest.

The number assembled, and which remained with the army, has been variously estimated, the figures running from fifteen hundred to three thousand. Stedman, an officer under Cornwallis, in his *History of the American War,* Vol. I., page 182, states "the army of the loyalists consisted of about eighteen hundred men," which I am inclined to think is about correct, though Edmund Burke states that after his defeat General MacDonald admitted he had three thousand.

There appears to be pretty strong evidence that in the host there was division and even conflicting claims and various opinions almost from the commencement of the enterprise to the final overthrow.

While at Cross Creek it was found very difficult to organize and arrange the companies, regiments, and precedence of rank so as to give general satisfaction and secure harmonious coöperation. Those who had been militia officers expected to hold the same rank in the army; and, on this principle there were too many officers for the requisite complement of men. The officers, and others who had lately arrived from Scotland, were called "new comers," and "new Scotch," and looked upon with jealousy by the rest. Those who had been born in this country or had been long residents were unwilling to have the "new comers" promoted over them. General MacDonald was forced to exercise all his wisdom and patience in tracing back their family standing and inquiring into their respective qualifications before making a decision. To give entire satisfaction was an impossible task. Some were so highly offended, at what they considered an injustice, and others failing to see such necessary discipline as would be conducive to success, that they withdrew and soon after joined the provincials. Nor was this the only disturbing element, for it had been given out that the governor was at Campbelton with a thousand British regulars to receive them, and this report had accelerated their movements. On approaching their encampment they saw the statement was without foundation, and large numbers turned their faces homeward. Having thus been deceived, the Regulators lost confidence in all other representations made by their leaders, and in consequence hundreds retired.

Amidst the dissensions and discouragements, Flora MacDonald arose equal to the emergency, and threw the weight of her character, influence, and oratory into the scale. On the public square, near the royal standard, in Gaelic, she made a powerful address, with all her power, exhibiting her genius she dwelt at length upon the loyalty of the Scotch, their bravery, and the sacrifices her people had made. She urged them to duty, and was successful in exciting all to a high military pitch. When she had concluded, the piper asked her what tune he should play. Like a flash she replied, "Give them leather breeches," which was probably suggested by the Scots wearing buckskin breeches, rolled up at the bottoms.

The movements of the Highlanders and Regulators were carefully watched by the patriots, though much had been done in great secrecy; but the passing of armed men could not well be effectually concealed.

Cross Creek had been greatly disturbed for months. In the midst of the loyalists there were a few sterling patriots. Robert Rowan, in the early stages of the movement, had formed an independent company, and determined to find out the action of the community. He was thus early prepared to give notice of what was in motion.

When the hosts began to move to their standards, swift messengers were immediately despatched to give warning to the patriot leaders. At Salisbury the district Committee of Safety met on February 6 and gave orders to the county committees to embody the militia and minute men and send them forward. Three days later the Tryon committee directed that each captain should detail one-third of the effective men in his district and march to suppress the insurrection. Everywhere the country was alarmed and thoroughly aroused. At the west, the forces were collected at Charlotte, Salisbury, and Hillsboro. On the tenth the committee at New Bern directed Colonel Richard Caswell to march immediately, and the colonels of Dobbs, Johnston, Pitt, and Craven counties were ordered to join Caswell with their troops. The patriot forces in Mecklenberg, Rowan, Granville, Bute, Surry, Guilford, Orange, and Chatham were hurried to the scene of action.

A messenger reached Wilmington on the ninth. Colonel James Moore at once issued orders to prepare to march against the insurgents. For eighty hours there was severe, unremitting labor in making preparations. Colonel Moore moved toward Cross Creek, being joined en route by the Bladen militia. Colonel Alexander Lillington and Colonel John Ashe were soon in the field. Nearly nine thousand men were in motion, and all the rest were ready to turn out at a moment's notice. It was determined to crush out the rebellion without delay.

The loyalists of Surry were speedily dispersed. In Guilford, Colonel James Martin assembled the patriots at the "Cross Roads," but the loyalists passed on. A company of which Samuel Devinny, one of the former Regulators, was the head, being opposed by Captain Dent, killed him. It thus appears that Captain Dent was the first in North Carolina to fall in the contest.

The rising of the Highlanders at the time appointed was ill-advised, and showed a want of judgment on the part of Governor Martin. The object of marching the Highlanders to Wilmington was to act in conjunction with a British fleet. At the very moment of the assembling of the Highlanders the fleet was still in Cork, Ireland, and remained there until February 12, and did not arrive at the Cape Fear until May 3. Even if the Highland army, under the circumstances, had reached Wilmington, it would have fared more disastrously than its defeat at the Widow Moore's Creek Bridge.

Deserted by the Regulators, and the Americans swarming around him, General MacDonald found it to be necessary to take his departure before the time appointed. Stedman, in his *History of the American War,* has pointed out that MacDonald had decided to avoid all conflict, and to gain the sea coast with the least possible cost. That he did not intend to act offensively is proved from the fact that at Rockfish the Americans occupied an unsoldierly position and one that would provoke an attack. On their left was a morass with a deep swamp, the northwest of the river on the right, and the deep creek of the Rockfish to the rear—all of which invited annihilation. This position must have been known to many in MacDonald's army. Then, again, the original position of the Americans at Moore's Creek Bridge was almost equally as dangerous, and if MacDonald had charged on his arrival there, victory would have been easily won. Fortunately, however, the insecurity of the position did not escape the vigilance of Colonel Caswell, and as soon as night came he retreated over the bridge.

The Highland army at Cross Creek was neither prepared for battle nor for the march, despite all the exertions General MacDonald had put forth. The armament was as good as could be desired under the circumstances and did not lack in baggage and magazine wagons.

On February 18, the Highland army took up its line of march for Wilmington, and as the regiments filed out of Cross Creek, Flora MacDonald reviewed them from under an oak tree, still standing on Cool Spring Street. Then mounting her snow-white charger, she rode up and down the marching columns, and animated them in the most cheerful manner. She had staked much on that army. There was her husband, Allen, with the rank of major; her son, Alexander, a captain, and her son-in-law, Alexander MacLeod, a colonel. The soldiers were

in high glee, and as they passed along, with drums beating, pipes play-
ing, and flags flying, they sang their old Scotch songs and rehearsed
the stories of their native land.

South of Cross Creek is a small stream called Rockfish, which
flows into Cape Fear River. Two roads lead from Cross Creek to Wilmington, one called the Brunswick road, the other the Negro Head
Point Road. The Brunswick Road crosses Rockfish Creek, which was
selected by General MacDonald for his route to Wilmington. After
marching four miles, General MacDonald went into camp, on account
of the American forces in his front.

Flora MacDonald continued with the army until it reached the
brow of Haymount, near the site of the old United States Arsenal,
where it encamped for one night. In the morning when the army took
up the line of march midst banners streaming in the breeze and
martial music floating in the air, Flora took her departure. It was with
great difficulty that her husband obtained her consent to return, reason-
ing that his life was enough to put in jeopardy. Having consented,
she embraced her husband, her eyes dimmed with tears, she uttered a
fervent prayer for his safety and speedy return to Killiegrey; she
mounted her snow-white horse, rode along the columns of the army,
encouraging the men, then retraced, and was soon in Cross Creek,
accompanied by Malcolm MacKay, aged sixteen. The first night she
spent with Mrs. MacKay, Malcolm's mother, near Longstreet. From
there she went to Killiegrey, in Anson County, where she remained
until the estate was confiscated by the Americans, when she removed
to a plantation on Little River belonging to Kenneth Black. This continued to be her residence until she left America. She made frequent
visits to Cross Creek until her final removal.

General James Moore, anticipating the movements of the Highland army, with great celerity moved up the Cape Fear, and took possession of Rockfish bridge, on the fifteenth, and then held the pass and
fortified his camp. There he was immediately joined by Robert Rowan
with sixty men from Cross Creek, and later by Lillington, Ashe, and
Kenan with the Duplin militia, increasing the whole number to fifteen
hundred. In the meanwhile Colonel Thackston and Colonel Alexander

Martin were rapidly approaching from the west with still larger re-enforcements.

On the nineteenth the royalists were paraded with a view to assail General Moore on the following night. A bare suspicion that such a prospect was contemplated was a sufficient cause for some of Colton's men to run off with their arms. This condition of affairs alarmed General MacDonald. However, the same day he sent General Moore the following:

HEADQUARTERS, FEBRUARY 19, 1776.

SIR: I herewith send the bearer, Donald Morrison, by advice of the Commissioners appointed by his Excellency, Josiah Martin, and in behalf of the army now under my command, to propose terms to you as friends and countrymen. I must suppose you unacquainted with the Governor's Proclamation, commanding all his Majesty's loyal subjects to repair to the King's royal standard, else I should have imagined you would, ere this, have joined the King's army, now engaged in his Majesty's service. I have therefore thought it proper to intimate to you, that, in case you do not, by twelve o'clock to-morrow, join the Royal standard, I must consider you as enemies, and take the necessary steps for the support of legal authority.

I beg leave to remind you of his Majesty's speech to his Parliament, wherein he offers to receive the misled with tenderness and mercy, from motives of humanity. I again beg of you to accept the proferred clemency. I make no doubt but you will show the gentleman sent on this message every possible civility; and you may depend in return, that all your officers and men which may fall into our hands shall be treated with an equal degree of respect.

I have the honor to be, in behalf of the army, sir, your most obedient, humble servant,   DONALD MCDONALD.

To the Commanding Officer at Rockfish.

P. S. His Excellency's Proclamation is herewith enclosed.

Knowing that Colonel Martin and Colonel Thackston were nearing the neighborhood, and wishing to gain time, General Moore thus replied to the missive:

CAMP AT ROCKFISH, FEBRUARY 19, 1776.

SIR: Yours of this day I have received; in answer to which, I must inform you, that the terms which you are pleased to say, in behalf of the army under your command, are offered to us as friends and countrymen, are such as neither my duty nor inclination will permit me to accept, and which I must presume you too much of an officer to expect of me. You were very right when you supposed me unacquainted with the Governor's Proclamation; but as the terms therein proposed are such as I hold incompatible with the freedom of Americans, it can be no rule of conduct for me. However, should I not hear further from you before twelve o'clock to-morrow, by which time I shall have an opportunity of consulting my officers here, and perhaps, Colonel Martin, who is in the neighborhood of Cross Creek, you may expect a more particular answer; meantime, you may be assured that the feelings of humanity will induce me to show that civility to such of you as may fall into our hands, as I am desirous should be observed towards those of ours who may be unfortunate enough to fall into yours.

I am, sir, your most obedient and very humble servant,

JAMES MOORE.

On the succeeding day General Moore sent the following to General MacDonald:

CAMP AT ROCKFISH, FEBRUARY 20, 1776.

SIR: Agreeable to my promise of yesterday, I have consulted the officers under my command, respecting your letter, and am happy in finding them unanimous in opinion with me. We consider ourselves engaged in a cause the most glorious and honorable in the world, the defense of the liberties of mankind, in support of which, we are determined to hazard everything dear and valuable; and in tenderness to the deluded people under your command, permit me, sir, through you, to inform them, before it is too late, of the dangerous and destructive precipice on which they stand, and to remind them of the ungrateful return they are about to make for their favorable reception in this country. If this is not sufficient to recall them to the duty which they owe to themselves and their posterity, inform them that they are engaged in a cause in which they cannot succeed, as not only the whole force of this country, but that of our neighboring provinces, is exerting, and now actually in motion to suppress them, and which must end in their utter destruction. Desirous, however, of avoiding the effusion of human blood, I have thought proper to send you a copy of the test recommended by the Continental Congress, which, if they will yet subscribe and lay down their arms, by twelve o'clock to-morrow, we are willing to receive them as friends and countrymen. Should this offer be rejected, I shall consider them as enemies to the constitutional liberties of America, and treat them accordingly.

I cannot conclude without reminding you, sir, of the oath which you and some of your officers took at New Berne, on your arrival in this country, which I imagine you will find difficult to reconcile to your present conduct. I have no doubt that the bearer, Captain James Walker, will be treated with proper civility and respect in your camp.

I am, sir, your most obedient and humble servant,

J. MOORE.

General MacDonald took occasion to answer the communication of General Moore in the following language:

HEADQUARTERS, FEBRUARY 20, 1776.

SIR: I received your favor by Captain James Walker, and observed your declared sentiments of revolt, hostility, and rebellion to the King, and to what I understand to be the constitution of this country. If I am mistaken, further consequences must determine; but while I continue in my present sentiment, I shall consider myself embarked in a cause which must, in its consequences, extricate this country from anarchy and licentiousness. I cannot conceive that the *Scots* emigrants, to whom I imagine you allude, can be under greater obligations to this country than to that of England, under whose gracious and merciful government they alone could have been enabled to visit this western region; and I trust, sir, it is in the womb of time to say, that they are not that deluded and ungrateful people which you would represent them to be. As a soldier in his Majesty's service, I must inform you, if you are yet to learn, that it is my duty to conquer, if I cannot reclaim, all those who may be hardy enough to take up arms against the best of Masters, as of Kings.

I have the honor to be, in behalf of the army under my command, sir, your most obedient servant,

To James Moore, Esq.   DONALD MCDONALD.

General MacDonald was fully aware that he could not put his threat into execution, for he had been informed that the minute-men were gathering in swarms around him; that Colonel Caswell at the head of the minute-men of Newbern, nearly eight hundred strong, were marching through Duplin County to effect a junction with General Moore, and that his communications with the seacoast had been cut off. Realizing the extremity of his danger, he resolved to avoid an engagement, and leave the army at Rockfish in his rear, and by celerity of movements, and crossing rivers at unexpected places, to disengage himself from the larger bodies and fall upon the command of Colonel Caswell. Before marching he exhorted his men to fidelity, expressed bitter scorn for the "base cravens who had deserted the night before," and concluded by saying, "If any amongst you are so faint-hearted as not to serve with the resolution of conquering or dying, this is the time to declare themselves." The speech was answered by a general huzza for the king, but from Cotton's corps of Regulators, two companies marched off the field and returned to their homes. The army decamped at midnight, retraced their steps and crossed the river at Campbelton. About daylight, on the morning of the twenty-first, the army, with the baggage having been landed on the north side, destroyed or sunk the boats, to prevent the pursuit of the enemy, and then resumed its march, sending a party fifteen miles in advance to secure the bridge over South River from Bladen into Hanover, pushing with rapid pace over swollen streams, rough hills, and deep morasses, hotly pursued by General Moore.

Perceiving the purpose of the enemy, General Moore instantly put in execution every precaution. He sent off an express to Colonel Caswell directing him to return and take possession of Corbett's Ferry over Black River, for the purpose of harassing the enemy, and impeding its progress. Thackston and Martin were to hold possession of Cross Creek and prevent a retreat in that direction, and Lillington and Ashe were ordered to make a forced march, and, if possible, reinforce Colonel Caswell, and if that could not be done, then to take possession of the Widow Moore's Creek Bridge, on the same road but nearer Wilmington. Apprehending that the enemy might attempt to pass through Duplin, pursuing a route to the eastward, the bridges of that county were in part destroyed, Colonel Cray holding back Salter's company for that purpose, and all the inhabitants held themselves ready to demolish the remainder if necessary to obstruct the march of the loyalists. At Wilmington, Colonel Purviance prepared to arrest the boats should the enemy descend the river, and with this intent threw a boom across the stream at Mount Misery, four miles above the town, and there stationed one hundred and twenty men, while another detachment held the pass at Heron's Bridge, ten miles out on the northeast branch.

Having dispatched his orders, General Moore, with the remainder of his army, hastened to Elizabethtown, hoping to strike MacDonald on his route to Corbett's Ferry, or else to fall on his rear and surround him at the river before he could cross. On the twenty-fourth, Moore crossed the Cape Fear; but having learned that Colonel Caswell was almost entirely out of provisions, he was compelled to wait there until the evening of the next day for a supply. Here he received a dispatch from Colonel Caswell informing him that the enemy had raised a flat, which had been sunk, about five miles above him, and had made a bridge by which the whole army had passed over. On receiving this intelligence, General Moore moved down the river in boats to Dollerson's Landing, about sixty miles, and thence to Moore's Creek, ten miles from the landing. On the twenty-sixth he arrived at Dollerson's in the afternoon.

Caswell, realizing the purpose of the enemy, changed his own course in order to intercept the march. On the twenty-third, General MacDonald thought to outwit him, and arraying the Highlanders in order of battle, with eighty able-bodied men, armed with broadswords, forming the center of the army; but Caswell, being posted at Corbett's Ferry, could not be reached for want of boats. Again the royalists were in extreme danger, but at a point six miles higher up the Black River they succeeded in crossing in a broad, shallow boat, while Mac-Lean and Fraser were left with a few men, and a drum and fife, to amuse Caswell.

Lillington, on the twenty-fifth, took possession of Widow Moore's Creek Bridge; and on the next day Caswell reached the west side, threw up a slight embankment, and destroyed a part of the bridge. A royalist, who had been sent into his camp under pretext of summoning him to return to his allegiance, brought back the information that Caswell had halted on the same side of the river as themselves, and could be assaulted to advantage. Caswell was both a good woodsman and a man of superior ability, and believing that he had misled the enemy, marched his column to the east side of the stream, removed the planks from the bridge, greased the sleepers with soft soap and tallow, and then placed his men behind trees and such embankments as could be thrown up during the night. The force amounted to a thousand men, consisting of the Newbern minute-men, the militia of Craven, Dobbs, Johnston, and Wake counties, besides the detachment under Lillington. The men of the Neuse region, their officers wearing silver crescents upon their hats, inscribed with the words, "Liberty or Death," were in front. The situation of the Highlanders was again perilous, for while facing this army, Moore, with his regulars, was close upon their rear.

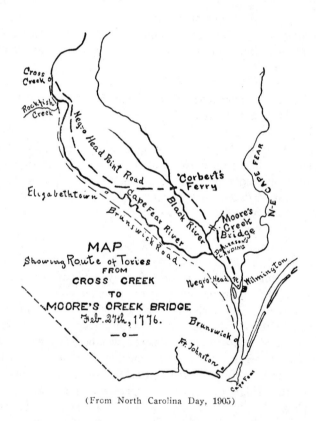

(From North Carolina Day, 1905)

CHAPTER VIII.

Battle of Widow Moore's Creek Bridge.

The Highland army was in a position where it could neither advance nor retreat. General MacDonald had proved himself fertile in resources; but it was now doomed to be deprived of his guiding hand, and those left to direct the army were not equal to the emergencies. The general was taken very ill and confined to his bed, and had been left at a house some eight miles from the scene of action, and this calamity was the precursor of a still heavier one about to fall like a thunderbolt. The Highlanders had been out-maneuvered, and the patriots had gained an advantageous position, forcing the enemy either to fight or else to take a course which would bring on them the imputation of cowardice and disconcert their plans.

On the evening before the battle a council of war was held, presumably in the presence of General MacDonald, the main object of which was to decide the question whether they should force their way through their adversaries, or determine some other movement. All the old and experienced officers, among whom was Colonel Donald MacLeod, then in command, both by priority of rank and common consent, were strongly opposed to battle, contending that the difficulty and danger of forcing their way in the face of an enemy, two-thirds their number, so strongly posted, defended by their entrenchments, mounted with two pieces of artillery and protected in front by a stream that was impassable except by a narrow bridge, which could be raked by their guns, were too great to be attempted. Besides, on good authority, it had been learned that by making a detour of only a few miles, the stream could be crossed where they could fight on equal grounds. These considerations, so sound and appealing to military science, were sneered at by others, and especially the young, self-conceited, and hot-headed MacLean, adventurous, spirited, self-willed, emphatically demanded courageous action. "Well," exclaimed MacLeod, as he closed the council, "at dawn to-morrow we will prove who is the coward."

Colonel MacLeod determined upon an early attack, and at one o'clock on the morning of the twenty-seventh, began his march, but owing to the time lost in passing an intervening morass, it was within an hour of daylight when they reached the west bank of the creek. Seventy men were selected, of the stoutest and most resolute in the army, and formed into a company under the command of Captain John Campbell, who were to have the post of greatest danger. They were to rush over the bridge in front of the army and storm the works, sword in hand. The fate of this company was the most important, for on it depended the issue of battle.

The Highlanders advanced through the open pine woods on a slope of descending ground, their officers well dressed in gay regimentals, banners and plumes waving in the breeze, and all marching in good order but with quick step to the sound of their pibrochs, while the thrilling notes of the bugle were heard in the distance, making a formidable appearance. Without resistance they entered the ground; but seeing Caswell's forces on the opposite bank, they reduced their columns and formed the line of battle in the woods. Their rallying cry was "King George and broadswords," and the signal of attack was three cheers, the drum to beat, and the pipes to play. While it was still dark MacLeod, accompanied by Captain John Campbell on his right, with a party of about forty of the swordsmen, advanced and at the bridge was challenged by one of the sentinels asking, "Who goes there?" He answered, "A friend." "A friend of whom?" "To the king." Upon this the sentinels bowed their faces down to the ground. MacLeod, thinking they might be some of his own command who had crossed the bridge, challenged them in Gaelic, but receiving no reply, fired his own piece, and ordered his party to fire also. All that remained of the bridge were the two pine sleepers, stripped of their bark and well greased.

The night before the battle, Colonel Caswell received information of the contemplated attack. This put him on his guard, and he made his arrangements accordingly. Lillington's men were drawn up across the peninsula, and lay on their arms all night. One of the pieces of artillery, known among the soldiers as "Mother Covington," a special favorite of the men, was placed in a position to command the bridge.

Colonel MacLeod and Captain Campbell rushed upon the sleepers of the bridge and succeeded in getting over. The Highlanders that followed had difficulty in keeping on the sleepers, some supporting themselves by thrusting their swords into the logs, and others falling into the muddy stream below. Lillington gave the command to fire, and the musketry swept the bridge. At last "Mother Covington" let go, with terrible effect. MacLeod was mortally wounded, but was seen to rise repeatedly from the ground, waving his sword and encouraging his men to come on, until twenty-six balls had penetrated his body. Campbell was shot dead, and at the same moment a party of militia under Lieutenant Ezekiel Slocum, who had forded the creek and penetrated a swamp on its western bank, fell suddenly upon the rear of the royalists. The loss of their leader, and the unexpected attack upon the rear, threw them into confusion, when all broke and fled.

There were probably twenty who got over the bridge, but all were killed or wounded, all of whom belonged to Campbell's company. Among them were Duncan MacRae, William Stewart, Kenneth Murchison, Laughlin Bethune, Murdoch MacRae, Alexander Campbell, and John MacArthur, of whom the three last were taken to Wilmington the next morning, and all died of their wounds within a week. There was among them a man from Cross Creek, by the name of Campbell, called in Gaelic "Far-earst," who by a desperate kind of valor, rushed over the bridge, but had hardly set his foot on the ground when his body was literally riddled by the rifle balls and he fell dead on the spot. MacLean survived his wound and in after life became sedate and saddened over the fate of MacLeod.

The Highlanders lost about seventy killed and wounded, while the patriots had none killed and two wounded, one of whom recovered. The victory was complete, decisive, and lasting, for the power of the Highlanders was completely broken. There fell into the hands of the Americans eight hundred and fifty prisoners, fifteen hundred rifles, all of them excellent pieces, three hundred and fifty guns and shot-bags, two hundred and fifty swords and dirks, two medicine chests, fresh from England, one of which was valued at £300 sterling, thirteen wagons with horses, which proved of great value to the slender supplies of the provincial forces. Besides all this, there was found secreted in a stable at Cross Creek, a box of guineas amounting to $75,000.

Some of the Highlanders escaped from the field of carnage by breaking down their wagons and riding away, three upon a horse. Many of those taken confessed they were forced and persuaded against their inclinations into the service. All the soldiers taken were disarmed and ordered to return to their homes immediately.

The American officers fully realized the importance of capturing all the leaders, for then the Highlanders would remain inactive in their homes. Hence, various companies were sent out to scour the country and apprehend every one who held rank in the army. On the following day General Donald MacDonald was taken prisoner. He was sitting on a stump and as his captors came up, he waved his commission, perhaps for the reason of being identified and humanely treated. There is a tradition that some of his soldiers surrounded his tent, and in desperation fought in his defense until driven off. Nearly all the chief men were taken the same day, including Allen MacDonald of Kingsburgh, and his son, Alexander.

It is possible that this account may fall to some who are descended from one or more of the prisoners, and, to others related to the victors; hence the completeness of this victory may be seen by giving a partial list of the prisoners, taken from a report of the committee of the Provincial Congress, April 20 and May 10, on the guilt of the Highland and Regulator officers then confined in the jail of Halifax. The prisoners were divided into four classes, namely:

First. Prisoners who had served in Congress.

Second. Prisoners who had signed Tests or Associations.

Third. Prisoners who had been in arms without such circumstances.

Fourth. Prisoners under suspicious circumstances.

The Highlanders coming under these various designations are given in the following order:

Farquhard Campbell, Cumberland county.

Alexander McKay, capt. of thirty-eight men, Cumberland county.

Alexander MacDonald (Condrach), Major of a regiment.

Alexander Morrison, Captain of a company of thirty-five men.

Alexander McDonald, son of Kingsborough, a volunteer, Anson county.

James McDonald, Captain of a company of twenty-five men.

Alexander McLeod, Captain of a company of thirty-two men.

John MacDonald, Captain of a company of forty men.

Alexander McLeod, Captain of a company of sixteen men.

Murdoch McAskell, Captain of a company of thirty-four men.

Alexander McLeod, Captain of a company of sixteen men.

Angus McDonald, Captain of a company of thirty men.

Neill McArthur, Freeholder of Cross Creek, Captain of a company of fifty-five men.

Francis Frazier, Adjutant to General McDonald's Army.

John McLeod, of Cumberland county, Captain of a company of thirty-five men.

John McKinzie, of Cumberland county, Captain of a company of forty-three men.

Kennith MacDonald, aid-de-camp to General MacDonald.

Murdoch McLeod, of Anson county, Surgeon to General Mac-Donald's Army.

Donald McLeod, of Anson county, lieutenant in Captain Morrison's company.

Norman McLeod, of Anson county, ensign in James McDonald's company.

John McLeod, of Anson county, lieutenant in James McDonald's company.

Laughlin MacKinnon, freeholder in Cumberland county, Lieutenant in Col. Rutherford's corps.

James Munroe, freeholder in Cumberland county, Lieutenant in Captain McRey's company.

Donald Morrison, Ensign to Captain Morrison's company.

John McLeod, Ensign to Capt. Morrison's company.

Archibald McEachern, Bladen county, Lieutenant to Capt. McArthur's company.

Rory McKinnon, freeholder, Anson county, volunteer.

Donald McLeod, freeholder, Cumberland county, Master to two regiments, General McDonald's Army.

Donald Stuart, Quarter Master to Col. Rutherford's Regiment.

Allen MacDonald, of Kingsborough, freeholder of Anson county, Col. of Regiment.

Duncan St. Clair.

Daniel McDaniel, Lieutenant to Seymore York's company.

Alexander McRaw, freeholder, Anson county, Capt. of a company of forty-seven men.

Kenneth Stuart, Lieutenant, Capt. Stuart's company.

Collin McIver, Lieutenant, Capt. Leggate's company.

Alexander MacLaine, Commissary to General MacDonald's Army.

Angus Campbell, Captain of a company of thirty men.

Alexander Stuart, Captain of a company of thirty men.

Hugh McDonald, Anson county, volunteer.

John McDonald, common soldier.

Daniel Cameron, common soldier.

Daniel McLean, freeholder, Cumberland county, Lieutenant to Angus Campbell's company.

Malcolm McNeill, recruiting agent for General MacDonald's Army, accused of using compulsion.

Some of the prisoners were discharged soon after their arrest, by signing a proper oath not to bear arms against the United States.

Most of the prominent characters among both the Highlanders and Regulators, some of whom had not been in the battle, but considered to be dangerous to the best interests of the province, were made prisoners and remanded for trial. Among these were Thomas Rutherford and Farquhard Campbell, men of intelligence, wealth, and influence. Both were members of the first convention of August 25, 1774; members of the second convention, signed the articles of Association, April 3, 1775; members of the first Congress which met in August, 1775. Their votes were in unison with the rest, but all the time kept up a good understanding with the royalists. For a day or two before the battle at Moore's Creek, Campbell was with General MacDonald giving information and advice, and the next day with Caswell for the same purpose, and was actually present with him during the engagement, making suggestions and pretending a deep interest in the fortunes of the day.

There are still many interesting incidents detailed concerning the flight of some who took part in the battle. There were others which taught the Americans to be constantly on their guard. Among those narrated is the action of Colonel Reid and Captain Cunningham, who, with a party of fourteen, after the battle, surprised a company of provincials at Cross Creek, disarmed them and then made their way to Fort Johnson.

CHAPTER IX.

RESULTS OF THE BATTLE.

It is the design not to enter into a free discussion of the important results accruing from the defeat of the Highlanders at Moore's Creek, nor follow up details of acts, however interesting they may be. There are certain historical matters which should be adverted to. As this battle was the first fought on North Carolina soil during the American Revolution, it would have results that might be far-reaching in their consequences.

On the Americans the victory had a most potent effect. It animated them with hope, established confidence, increased valor, and kindled the flames of patriotism. An enthusiastic patriot, writing under date of March 10, 1776, says: "It is inconceivable to imagine what joy this event has diffused through this province; the importance of which is heightened by Clinton and Lord William Campbell's being now in Cape Fear. How amazingly mortified must they prove in finding that this weak, poor, and insignificant Carolina, in less than fifteen days, could turn out more than ten thousand independent gentlemen volunteers, and within that time pursue them to the very scene of action. Since I was born I never heard so universal an ardor for fighting prevail and so perfect a union among all classes of men."

True to their profession, the leaders of the patriots determined to treat the Highlanders in general with the utmost consideration. This fact Stedman clearly recognizes, for he records that Colonel Moore and Colonel Caswell "behaved with great leniency and moderation towards the loyalists while they continued in power."

The defeat of this army disconcerted the plans of Governor Martin, but he adhered to the idea that if a considerable force should penetrate into the interior, thousands of loyalists would flock to the royal standard. Even Cornwallis showed the same idea as late as 1781, when he marched his army into Cross Creek. The loyalists, though disheartened, generally remained faithful to the crown, but disarmed and deprived of their leaders, the Highlanders had not the heart again to enter the army. They had also taken a parole which nearly all kept inviolate.

During the whole course of the war, the Highlanders were regarded with suspicion, probably caused by unruly spirits among them. The Americans did not rest matters simply by confining the officers, but every precaution was taken to overcome them, not only by their parole, but also by armed force, for a militia company at once was stationed at Cross Creek until November 21. On July 28, 1777, it was reported that the royalists were in motion, which aroused the Americans to arms and a vigilant watch was kept over those at Cross Creek. So, also, the Highlanders were kept in alarm. In June, 1776, it was reported among them that a company of light horse was coming into the settlement, and every one thought he was the man wanted, and hence all hurried to the swamps and other fastnesses in the forest. From the poor Highland women, who had lost father, husband, brothers in battle, or whose men-folk were imprisoned in the jail at Halifax there went up such a wail of distress as to cause the Provincial Congress to put forth a proclamation, ordered to be printed into the "Erse tongue," in which it was declared that they "warred not with those helpless females, but sympathized with them in their sorrow," and recommended them to the "bounty of those who had aught to spare from their necessities."

The district in which the Highlanders were settled was in a tumult for some time after the battle at Moore's Creek. Colonel Caswell marched through the district, but allowed no violence, trying in all cases to be just. But there were independent parties who committed outrages, of which the legal officers were guiltless. There was much suffering caused by the lawless. These inhuman acts were deplored by all the better class, but owing to the disordered state of society, such things were often beyond their control. Then the people were aggravated by the acts of British agents who kept up the turmoil. Hector MacNeill and Archibald Douglas, of the British army, came into the district and tried to exert an influence over the people, declaring the British had money to any amount; that they would conquer the country, and that the Scotch would be handsomely rewarded if found on the king's side. Again the Highlanders began to embody, and from that time until the close of the war, the country presented a terrible scene of bloodshed, devastation, and ruin.

From the opening to the close of the Revolution, there were Highlanders in North Carolina enrolled in both the contending forces. Those on the British side were mostly recent emigrants, the bulk of whom were not familiar with the English language. Some, however, were with the patriots, and fought with Marion and other commanders. Those Highlanders belonging to earlier emigrations were principally loyal to their adopted country. The contentions of the same race, each party striving for mastery would naturally provoke the most severe animosities.

The act of the insurgents of 1776 enrolled in General MacDonald's army is sometimes called "The Insurrection of the MacDonalds." During and after the war these people, to a great number, withdrew from the State, some returning to Scotland, and others settled in Nova Scotia.

It will not be necessary, in this connection, to follow the history of the officers imprisoned in Halifax jail. I have already done that in my *Scotch Highlanders in America*. However we must present the final struggles of Allen and Flora MacDonald.

With other captured officers, Allen was closely confined in the jail at Halifax. On April 11, 1776, the North Carolina Provincial Congress resolved that Allen be admitted to his parole; that he should not go without the limits of the town of Halifax; that he should not correspond with any person who is inimical to American interests; that he shall not convey intelligence to such person; that he will take no plans or drafts while on parole, and that every day between the hours of ten and twelve o'clock he shall report to the officer of the guard.

According to a letter dated April 22, 1776, General Donald Mac-Donald, Colonel Allen MacDonald of Kingsburgh, his son, Alexander, Major Alexander MacDonald, besides fifteen captains, one lieutenant, and five minor officers, including the chaplain, Rev. John Bethune, all of the Highland army, were sent prisoners to Philadelphia.

On the way from North Carolina to Philadelphia, while resting at Petersburg, May 2, 1776, Kingsburgh wrote the following letter:

SIR: Your kind favor I had by Mr. Ugin (?), with the Virginian money enclosed, which shall be paid if ever I return, with thanks; if not, I shall take to order payment. Colonel Eliot who came here to receive the prisoners Confined the General and me under a guard and sentries to a Room; this he imputes to the Congress of North Carolina not letting Brigadier Lewes (who commands at Williamsburg) know of our being on parole by your permission when at Halifax. If any opportunity afford, it would add to our happiness to write something to the above purpose to some of the Congress here with directions (if such can be done) to forward said orders after us. I have also been depressed of the horse I held, and hath little chance of getting another. To walk on foot is what I never can do the length of Philadelphia. What you can do in the above different affairs will be adding to your former favors. Hoping you will pardon freedom, wrote in a hurry. I am with real Esteem and respect, Honorable Sir, your very obedient servt.   ALLEN MACDONALD.

On June 28, Kingsburgh was permitted, after signing a parole and word of honor, to go to Reading, in Berks County, Pennsylvania. At the same time the Committee of Safety

"*Resolved,* That such Prisoners from North Carolina as choose, may be permitted to write to their friends there; such letters to be inspected by this Committee, and the jailer is to take care that all the paper delivered in to the Prisoners be used in such Letters, or returned him."

The action of the Committee of Safety was approved by the Continental Congress, which, on July 9, 1776, "*Resolved,* That the committee of safety of Pennsylvania release Allan McDonald, of Kingsborough, a prisoner in the gaol of Philadelphia, on his parole, and that, upon his signing his parole, he be treated agreeable to former resolutions of Congress." His son was ordered released by Congress on the fifteenth by the following resolution: "*Resolved,* That Alexander McDonald, son of Captain McDonald, be liberated on his parole, and allowed to reside with his father."

On September 25, the Continental Congress received a report from the Committee on the Treasury, in which it is stated that there is due "to Colonel Allen McDonald of Kingsborough, and his son, Alexander McDonald, for their allowance of two dollars per week for 21 weeks, and for their servants' allowance, 21 weeks, at one dollar per week, settled to the 17th September, 105 dollars."

The time when Allen MacDonald was removed from Philadelphia to Reading, I have not been able to determine. He was removed to the latter place, where were confined Allen MacDonald, Sr., Allen MacDonald, Jr., Alexander MacDonald, Rennel MacDonald, and Archibald MacDonald, hostages from the Mohawk settlement, sent there by General Philip Schuyler.

On April 10, 1777. Congress received the following petition from Allen MacDonald:

The Petition of Capt: Allen McDonald of Kingsburgh, to John Hancock Esquire, in Congress.—Humbly Sheweth—

That whereas your Petitioner and Son, are now nigh fourteen Months Prisoners of War, and were above four Months of those, in close confinement, removed from one Gaol, to another, and different places of confinement, in North Carolina Virginia, & Maryland, till they arrived in Philadelphia, from there—they were admitted on Parole, to reside at Riading, in the County of Berks, where they now are. From whence I am hopefull, it will be certified by his Excellency General Mifflin, Commanding Officer there and the County Committee, that they kept closs to their Parole, without giving the smalest offence to any person whatever—

Your Petitioner begs leave further to observe, that Provision— Drink, Lodging, Cloathing, and in short every thing, is so extravagantly high priced, that Prisoners must be in a very miserable State, Two Dollars, the common allowance pr. Week, being of greater service, ten Months before now, than Six this day—From the above different circumstances; Your Petitioner expects, you will exchange him, & Son for Officers of the like denomination, or order them to New York on Parole, till duly Exchanged.—And in complying with either of the above requests; you will very much relieve and Oblige—
Sir—Your very Humble and Obedient Servant.
Riading, Aprile 5th, 1777.   ALLEN MCDONALD.

Petitioner hath not received even the small allowance of Two Dollars [word omitted] -eek, for himself, Son & Servant, from the 30th December last— [word torn off] received what was due till then, from his Excellency General Mifflin.
Endorsement: Petition. Capt. Allen McDonald of Kingsburgh—Prisoner on Parole in Riading.—

10 April, 1777, No. 8. Petition of Allen McDonnel
read 10 April 1777
referred to board of war

On June 10, 1777, the following was offered in Congress: "That General Washington be directed to propose an exchange of Lt. Colonel Allan McDonald and Lt. Alexander McDonald for such officers of equal Rank as are entitled to a priority of Exchange."

On July 22, 1777, Congress received the following from "Alexander (Allen) McDonald of Kingsborrow":

SIR: Some time passd, I petitioned Congress through your hands, in regard to my being exchanged, with my Son; which, His Excelency General Mifflin, was so good, as deliver you; Thereafter the Chairman of the Committee here, James Reid Esqr: wrott to some of the Members of Congress, that the voice of the People had made joice of Lt. Colonel Lutes [who was permited to come home on Parole by His Excelency Sir William Howe] as their Colonell, & represented me as the fittest Person to be Exchanged for him, through my good behaviour & Strict attention, with my Son, to our Parole [as they were pleased to term it] since we came here—No return being made to this, The whole Officers of the 4th: Battalion of Pensylvania Militia in a Body Signed a Petition to Congress, praying Colonell Lutes being released from the Secret tyes of his Parole, by exchanging him for me, for the above reasons, What, success this last Petition had, I have not yet learned, tho I fear, it shaired the same fate with the former—Now Sir, permit me to say; when you'll know, the dispersed, and distress't state of my family, you will, at least sympathize with me, and pity my oppress'd mind. I am here with one of my Sons Seventeen months a Prisoner— My Wife is in North Carolina 700 Miles from me in a very sickly tender State of health, with a younger Son, a Daughter, & four Grand Children—Two Sons in our Service of whom, I heared little or nothing, since one of them had been wounded in the Battle of Bunkers hill —And two in Britain, of whom I heared no accounts since I left it— Them in Carolina I can be of no service to in my present state, but were I Exchanged, I would be of service to the rest if in life, If not, with the assistance of the Almighty my mind wou'd be fix'd—Now Sir, let me further tell you, I am a Captain in the Regular Service, & my Son a Lieutenant, I rank as Lieut. Colonel of Militia in North Carolina; in this station I was made Prisoner, and I am convinced Sir William Howe will Exchange me in either of those Ranks—if not—I hereby binde my honor, my Character, & even my life, I, and my Son will returne—if Colonell Lutes is not to be exchanged, fix on whome you please of equal Rank, & a Lieut: for my Son; let me bring their names to General Howe & if they are not sent, we will upon Honour, & Conscience, return to our former Parole—-Here is Capt. Graydon of your regular Service come home with some other Gentlemen on Parole. Could not he be exchanged for me, & some Lieut: you please for my Son—Hopeing you'll pardon the anguish of an uneasy mind, and contribute to its relief, which is but Charity—I am with Respect Sir—

Your Very Humble—
and Obedient Servant—

Riading July 18th   Allen McDonald of Kingsborrow
    1777

To—

Address: The Honble. John Hancock President—
                of the Continental Congress—
                        Philadelphia—

Endorsement: Letter from Alex. McDonald
            of Kingsborrow 18 July 1777
            read 22
            referred to the board of war
            reported upon

On August 7, 1777, Congress received a report from the Auditor General, in which he states "that there is due to Allan McDonald, his son and servant, for their allowance as prisoners, from the 18 September, 1776, to the 5 August, 1777, being 46 weeks, the sum of 230 dollars."

Attempts were made to exchange the Highland prisoners on the part of General Washington, and others in authority, but as the captives were so unfortunate as to have no one to intercede for them among those at British headquarters, on August 21, 1777, Congress, in passing upon a report from the Board of War, *"Resolved,* That Allan McDonald, of Kingsborough, North Carolina, a captain in the British regular service, be permitted to go into New York to negotiate an exchange for himself and his son, a lieutenant in the same service; he to give his parole not to convey to the enemy or bring back any intelligence whatever of a political nature, and to return in a certain time to be fixed by his parole or when called for, on behalf of the United States."

Kingsburgh proceeded to New York. and during the month of

November succeeded in effecting his exchange, and was soon placed in command of a company of provincials.

From the "Letter-Book of Captain Alexander MacDonald of the Royal Highland Emigrants," we catch glimpses of Kingsburgh and his sons, with letters directed to him, here given in full, as they are of interest to all who may desire to know of Flora MacDonald's family :

HALIFAX (N. S.) 18 Oct., 1777.

DR Cousin : I am Extremely happy to hear that you & Y^r Son were safe at New York. I hope to have the further pleasure of seeing you both soon here in Case you should have Occasion or be at a loss for want of money I send you Inclosed the State of your Accot. from wch you can see how much you may Venture to draw for. If Major Donald McDonald* is there yet pray give him my kind Comp^{ts}. I should have wrote him long before now if I did not think he had Gone to England when Genl McLean left that place. I have seen a pretty lad here a Son of his L^t. of Marines. You may tell him he was very well and Expected soon to be in England. I dare say Ronald will write to you by this Opportunity they are very happy at the thoughts of Seeing you soon & for Gods Sake don't Stay long Come to us before the Winter sets in & bring all the fine fellows you possibly can get along with you but dont venture in anything less than a frigate. Give my kind Comp^{ts} to Sandy tho' a Stranger & am Dr Cousin.

Yrs Sincerely.

(*Brigadier-General Donald MacDonald, who commanded in North Carolina.)

HALIFAX, 31ST DECR, 1777.

DR Cousin : It is wth Sincere pleasure & Satisfaction I rec^d Yours of the 30th November Ult^o. You have surely wrote it in the Morning Early Else St. Andrew w^d have prevented the pleasure of my receiving a Letter from you of that date & Nothing can give me greater pleasure than to hear of you & Your Son being Safe out of the hands of the Rebels. I am also happy to hear of M^{rs}. Macdonald's Wellfare and her Spirited behaviour when bro^t before the Committee of Rascals in North Carolina.

I don't doubt but She & the Other Gentlewomen there will be sorely oppressed by the Savage Cruelty of those Wretches who at present has the Upper hand of them Tho' they may Sorely repent it before this War is at an End.

I had rather you was here at the head of your own Company in our Regiment than Commanding a Com^y of Provincials wch as we have a great many Enemys may be made a handle of to hinder our

Establishment. Major Small who goes by this Opportunity will talk to you more fully on this Subject. The Rank of the Officers of this Regm^t is already settled by Major Small & the rest of the Officers present upon the Spot. How far the Commission you speak of will avail you I do not know but I think Sandy McLeod B:M: did try to get rank from it when Frazier's Regim^t was raised last War but I believe Was refused however You'll be in the right to try it if ever the Regim^t be established if not it will not be worth your trouble.

I have all your Subsistance from the Date of your Commission to the 24th Feby, 1778, also your arrears and what Ba^g & fforage money has been allowed Since as the inclosed abstracts will Show, Your Son Sandys, as well as your own for which Sums or whate part of them you plese you and Sandy May Draw if you have not Drawn on me Allready to the amount of the Ballances in yours favours. You See I have Pay'd Some money on your account to Capt. Murdock Mc-Lean but Should it not be agreeable to you I have it still in my Power to recharge the Same to Capt McLaine, as he has a Chance to See you soon you will Settle matters and let me know. I would not advise you to venture here but in a man of warr and I assure you I think this part of British America the happiest Spot in it at present and would be very hapie to see you and all the othere officers of our Corp^ts here with all Cliver ffellows of recruits you can Bring with you—we want about 85 to Compleat but we Expect a Great Manney from Newfoundland and from your Endeavours—I hope Major Small will Sende Capt Alex^r Campbell to joine his Company or Oblidge him to Quitt, which I Darr Saie he will do for a triffle and I hope in that Case you will secure it for Sandy being the 2^d oldest Lieutt If there is no Certainty of our Establishment I am convinced Campbell will Rathere Give up the Company for Nothing rather than be obliged to joine at lest would be Glad to take one or two hundered pounds for it I mean the Company because (indeed) I would not think Safe to pay above one years purchass for it tho' I would be Sory that any body Eles Should purchass overy Sandys head.

As Your Son Ranald is going will be the Bearer of this I need not trouble you with any news to tell the truth there are none, only he will Give you a Description of the place he is a fine young ffellow and will make an Excellent Officer if he lieves—You tell me you have contracted a Great Deall of Debt, I Darr Saie you must have lieved Expensive but it is high time now my Dear Allan to Study Oeconomy your 3 oldest Sons are provided for Espetialy if this Reg^t will Establish^d therefore has no right to Expect any more assistance from you, if you was worth ten thousand a year Except when a purchass Came in their way.

I Darr Saie you and your Vollunteers make a formidable figure in the Dress you have Describ'd to Me which I perfectly understand all but the cuteikins which I take to be half Boots or Geatters.

I cannot Give you the lest accot of Poor Normand Talisker Some People told me he and his wife went home what to do there God only knows I Don't know that I felt more concerned for a man in my life than I have for him Curse the Grogg at lest too much of it. I'm hapy to hear poor John McLean and Peggy are unmollested, I wish they may continue so. Pray for Godsake is it possible to Gett M^{rs}. McDonald & the othere poor women from N. Carolina—I thought my worthy ffriende Major Donald McDonald had Gone to England long ago if this findes him with you pray offer him my most Humble respects.

Bring with you or Sende to us Some Syder & Aples of the Best Sort if they can be Gote if you can go with Safety to Staten island I wish you would be so Good as to Sende or order to be Sent Some Negro Chielderen that are at my House as their Mothere is Dead, unless you finde matters are like to be Sattled in which case I would let them Stay where they are I again wish we were alltogethere as the more we are in one place the more respectable our appearance wishing you and all ffriends the complments of the Season and with M^{rs}. McDonald's and my kinde wishes for every thing that can make you Hapy & ever I am with Sincerity and truth Dear Cousin

Yours affectionatly

A. M. D.

The third letter is dated

HALIFAX, 12TH, JANUARY, 1778.

DR COUSIN: Since my last of the 31st of Decem^r ult^o wch will be delivered to you by Your Son Ronald who from some hints I rec^d is going there not only wth Anxiety to see you but with some other Views to get you to lay out the little Money you have in my hands in purchasing a higher Commission for himself or Charles a Manuvre I w^d highly approve of if you could afford it, but I have already given a hint upon this head & I again tell you that I think y^r three sons extremely well provided for consigering their Age especially is this Reg^t be Established as I hope it is by this time. Ronald is already in a very good corps & pretty far advanced & probably may have a Chance for a Company before this work is at an End. Charles is a fine young fellow for whom I have the Sincerest regard but the income of a General Off^r w^d be rather small for him, if he could get it, he is very Sensible & very Clever when Sober but rather unhappy when he is any ways disguised in Liquor but y^r presence here might be the means of altering him & putting a Stop to it. These Circumstances are as galling to me to relate as they can possibly be to you to hear them but I think it my Duty from the Sincerest Friendship to acquaint you with them. Were so near Relations indifferent to me I might laugh as others do and pass it over in silence. I beg You w^d not let Ronald or Charles know any part of this intelligence but with the power & authority of a parent Command Ronald at his peril to tell you the truth of all he knows Concerning Charles & his Behaviour. I have nothing earthly to lay to his Charge but w^t the Effects of Liquor is the Cause of & a propensity to Extravagance wch I wish to God he was cured of As no man has a right to Spend more than his income & not even that it being much more honorable for a young Off^r to have a Guinea in his pocket to lend to his Comrade than to be obliged to borrow one from him & I beg you w^d keep a tight hand & learn them to live upon their pay Especially as you have other things to do with Y^r money & other people to provide for. In Short I wish you was here for several good Reasons. This will be delivered you by your old acquaintance Captn Murd^k McLean, a Sensible facetious clever honest worthy fellow. As its Supposed you are acquainted with all the Scotch folks in New York you will no doubt introduce Capt McLean to them all.

Wishing you a Speedy & Safe arrival here wth great Good news from the Southward I remain Dr Cousin

Y^{rs} Sincery.

The last letter is dated

HALIFAX, 19th feb^y, 1778.

The above is a Copy wch I intended to send by Captn Murd^k McLane but he departed in such a hurry that I could not get it finished. Since wch time I have nothing new to tell you only the Departure of our worthy Major who left us the 27th of January & hope is now Safe in London where he will insist upon the fate of our Regiment before he leaves it. So it is to be hoped that two months will Satisfy our Anxiety & curiosity.

I sent my two Eldest boys along with him to the Care of W^m. Macdonald of Edinburgh and to be sent to the Highlands for one or two Years if he approves of it.

I furnished your Son Ronald with five half Joannis wch I placed to your Acc^t as he expected to get an Order from you for that purpose & I was obliged within these few days to Accommodate Charles with above £50 Ster^g he has by the managem^t of your Comp^y the 3 contingent wch is equal to £27.9 Ster^g a year & £10 paid him out of your Baggage & Forrage Money by order of Major Small. If all this is not Suff^t to Support Char^s what will other poor Subalterns do who has not a farthing but their bare subsistance.

I understand that Charles and Ronald are entirely agst your Joining the Regiment. I dont know w^t good reason they can have for it but One thing I am sure of it is absolutely necessary that you should be as near them as possible to overawe their Conduct & assist them with your good Advice & without you clearly see that you can do better for yourself by staying where you are I w^d earnestly recommend it to you to Join the Reg^t as soon as possible with all the Offrs & Recruits you can possibly bring along with you As well for the above Reasons as for the Character of the Regim^t. As the more there are together of us the more Respectable Appearance we'll make & of Course the better Chance we'll have to compleat our wishes of Establishment.

Bad as this place was always reckoned This certainly the Most peaceable Corner now in America & if you can by any Means obtain a safe Conduct for Mrs. Macdonald & Mrs. McLeod you might order them to follow you to this place.

I have no more to add but to assure you that I am Dr Cousin
Y^r Real friend & hble Servant.

In a letter addressed to Gen. Francis MacLean, dated Halifax, July 5, 1778, Capt. Alexander Mac Donald speaks of a letter that the former had sent by Allen MacDonald, but the last named had not yet arrived. Reference is also made of the cash advanced by Gen. MacLean to Allen MacDonald and his thirty recruits. The last reference to Kingsburgh is in a letter dated Halifax, August 21, 1778, in which is the statement, "If Capt. Murd. McLean or Capt. Allan Macdonald Should be there (New York) tell them as I have said before it is very surprizing w^t keeps them there that I will Certainly Stop their Credit from receiving any more money if they dont Join the Reg^t or Assign Sufficient Reasons to the Contrary."

Just when Kingsburgh left New York for Halifax, Nova Scotia, I am unable to discover. It is, however, probable, some time during the autumn of 1778. He joined his regiment, the eighty-fourth, or Royal Highland Emigrant Regiment, Second Battalion, taking command of the Eighth Company, his commission dating from June 14, 1775. He was deprived of the rank assigned him by Governor Martin. The Second Battalion was commanded by Major John Small. About the close of 1778, the regiment received Establishment. The uniform was the full Highland garb, with purses made of raccoon skins. The officers wore the broadsword and dirk, and the men a half-basket sword. That part remaining in Nova Scotia saw but little service. Allen MacDonald remained with his regiment, without seeing any particular service, until its reduction in 1783, when he returned to Skye, as a captain on half pay. On his arrival at Portree, he was met by Flora, with a numerous party of friends, to welcome him. Immediately he set out for the estate of Kingsburgh, which during his absence in America, had been left open for his return.

As already noted, the son, Alexander, was released from imprisonment at the same time as the father, and the two proceeded together to New York. The next glimpse of Alexander we find him at Fort Edward, Nova Scotia, November 23, 1778. The next, he was put in command of the prize crew on board the *Ville de Paris,* and, together with his brother, Ranald, went down with that vessel, October 5, 1782. How Ranald reached the army I am not informed. It seems reasonable to assume he was not at the battle of the Widow Moore's Creek Bridge. From MacDonald's "Letter Book," it appears that Charles received, in 1776, a commission of lieutenant from Major Small, and was warmly recommended by Earl Percy.

MacKenzie, in his *History of the MacDonalds,* states that Flora's son, James, was "a brave officer, who served with distinction in Tarlton's British Legion," but does not mention the part performed by John.

CHAPTER X.

Flora MacDonald was soon aroused to the fact that the battle was disastrous to her and her immediate countrymen, and that her husband, a son, and her son-in-law were incarcerated in the jail at Halifax, North Carolina. Woes rapidly crowded upon her, all of which, in the spirit of a true heroine, she attempted to surmount. She was denied the privilege of visiting her husband and never saw him again in America.

War is the reverse of humanity. Its horrors have been pictured by the ablest pens. It arouses all the baser passions. Fortunately there are redeeming qualities. There are characters able to rise pre-eminent. There is no evidence that Flora MacDonald was ever bitter, vindictive, or unforgiving. In short, her character, from any view-point, is one to be admired. True, she was instrumental in bringing on the war, but she paid the penalty without a murmur and without a censure. The battle at Moore's Creek must have struck a knell of woe to her heart. All her sons were in the British service. Her only married daughter, Anne, was settled in a house of her own, and her daughter, Fanny, was still in precarious health from the dregs of a recent fever, and yet too young to sympathize in her mother's distress. The revolution around her was rapid and changing; plots and intrigues various; alarms constant, and every passing day placed her in a position where her mind hovered between hope and fear. Nor was this all. She was an object of suspicion, and her every movement was noted. Had she not been prominent in the rising of the Mac-Donalds? Had she not spoken words of encouragement to and exhorted the Highland army to be brave? Was it not reasonable to conclude that her interest and determination were still the same?

It would be but reasonable to assume that Flora MacDonald should suffer for what she had done, when the war spirit was dominant. True,

she was not arrested, nor imprisoned, nor, in person, was she molested.
But the purported evidence against her was so great, that she was
summoned before the Committee of Safety. True to her character,
during the examination she is said to have exhibited a "spirited behavior." She was permitted to return home in peace, but not so to
remain, for war produces lawlessness. Irresponsible parties, taking
advantage of the unsettled state of affairs, ravished her plantation and
pillaged her residence. As previously noted, her estate was confiscated
by the Act of November, 1777, passed by the Provincial Congress at
Newbern, when she sought a home on the plantation of old Kenneth
Black. If any person was seen in her company it was sufficient evidence that the party was disloyal to the cause of America. Added to
all her misery she was called to grieve the loss of a son and a daughter,
who died of typhus fever, aged respectively eleven and thirteen, buried
at Killiegrey. Their names have not been preserved. In after years
the kind-hearted proprietor of Killiegrey, Mr. Gray, fenced in the
graves, erected a small monument to mark the spot, and cared for the
same up to the breaking out of the Civil War, but now none of the
older citizens residing near the place, know anything about the location
of the graves.

Mistreatment was perpetrated on her daughters. Caruthers, in
his *Revolutionary Incidents,* has preserved an account of the massacre
at Piney Bottom, a branch of the Rockfish. Here Colonel Wade, returning home in a peaceable manner, with a few men to guard the
families with him, was surprised in the night by a large party of Tories,
who shot down five or six and then plundered the camp. Colonel Wade
immediately collected about one hundred dragoons. They came into
Richmond County, caught Daniel Patterson and whipped him until
he gave the names of all he knew who were at Piney Bottom. In
Moore County they caught quite a number and put them to death.
Some of the party came to old Kenneth Black's house. Both doors
being open, the men rode in until it was full of horses, and the family
were crowded into the chimney. Mr. Black's family having had the
smallpox, two daughters of Flora MacDonald, Mrs. Anne MacLeod
and Fanny, came over to see their friends; "but, to their utter surprise,
they found the Whigs there, who took the gold rings from their fingers

FLORA MAC DONALD'S SILVER
(From Bulletin 2, North Carolina Historical Commission)

and the silk handkerchiefs from their necks; then putting their swords into their bosoms, split down their silk dresses and, taking them out into the yard, stripped them of all their outer clothing." In the above account Caruthers has his date wrong, or else the incident confused with another.

Under all the adverse circumstances Flora continued calm, peaceful, and resigned in her demeanor.

Allen MacDonald managed to have a letter delivered to Flora, in which he advised her to return to the Isle of Skye. It was her desire to remain in America, though in distress and her means limited. She decided to comply with her husband's desire, and leave at the earliest opportunity. Owing to the scouts of the patriots it was a difficult matter to leave the country. But, happening to be at a social gathering, she met Captain Eben Ingram, an American officer, to whom she narrated her difficulties. He promised to use his good offices in her behalf, and soon after secured her a passport from Cross Creek to Wilmington. From thence she secured a passage by vessel to Charleston, South Carolina.

It appears to be well established that in order to secure money to defray her expense she sold her silverware. A silver tray, reputed to have been used for that purpose, was preserved in Wilson, North Carolina. Flora possessed a very large and handsome set of silver, probably presented her while a prisoner in London. While in Wilmington, perceiving she had not enough money for her journey, she was induced to part with it. This was purchased by Richard Quince. The waiter, bowl, ladle, and cream pitcher are now owned by Mrs. E. J. Justice, of Greensboro. Several other pieces are owned by Mrs. Brooke Empie, of Wilmington, and still others widely distributed. It would appear that public enterprise would place all in the State museum at Raleigh. As previously noted, Col. James MacQueen contributed largely, and it is more than probable that others rendered financial assistance.

Killiegrey was forcibly wrenched from Flora MacDonald, and long since the residence was destroyed by fire. Upon that home she had built her hopes and there anticipated spending her declining years. Whatever may have been her misfortunes, "her name is still held in reverence by the people of North Carolina, and especially by those who are descended from the Scotch settlers of the Cape Fear region. The memory of the Tory beauty, so brave-hearted, and yet so gentle and kind, is as fragrant as the pines among which she lived."

In 1779, accompanied by Fanny alone, still in ill health, of all the family, Flora MacDonald left Charleston on board a British vessel. Crossing the Atlantic the Scottish heroine met with another misfortune. The sloop in which she sailed encountered a French war vessel, and a contest ensued. During the engagement Flora refused to go below, but prominently appeared on deck. The courage of the men appearing to fail, she ascended the quarter-deck, during the fiercest of the battle, and encouraged them to more desperate conduct. She was thrown violently down during the affray and her left arm broken, yet she refused to leave her post, and continued to animate the sailors. She never left the deck until after the French had been beaten off. In after years she was accustomed to say that she had fought for both the House of Stewart and the House of Hanover, but had been worsted in the service of each.

On arriving in Scotland Flora immediately repaired to the residence of her brother in Milton, who erected for her a cottage, where she lived until her husband's return. Nothing of a special nature occurred during her sojourn at Milton. She visited her friends and kept up quite a correspondence with her acquaintances. Two of her letters have been preserved, addressed to the lady of Sir Alexander Muir Mackenzie, who had paid great attention to her son, Alexander, when he was a boy.

The first is as follows:

DUNVEGAN, SKYE, 12TH JULY, 1780.

DEAR MADAM: I arrived in Inverness the third day after parting with you, in good health, and without any accidents, which I always dread. My young squire continued always very obliging and attentive to me. I staid at Inverness for three days. I had the good luck to meet with a female companion from that to Skye. I was the fourth day, with great difficulty, at Raasay, for my hands being so pained with the riding.

I have arrived here a few days ago with my young daughter, who promises to be a stout Highland "Caileag," quite overgrown of her age. Nanny and her family are well. Her husband was not sailed the last account she had from him.

I have the pleasure to inform you, upon my arrival here, that I had two letters from my husband, the latter dated 10th of May. He was then in very good health, and informs me that my son Charles has got the command of a troop of horse in Lord Cathcart's regiment; but alas! I have heard nothing since I left you about my son Sandy, which you may be sure, gives me great uneasiness. But I still hope for the best.

By public and private news I hope we will soon have peace re-established, to our great satisfaction, which, as it's a thing long expected and wished for, will be for the utility of the whole nation, especially to poor me, that has my all engaged. Fond to hear news, · and yet afraid to get it.

I wait here till a favorable opportunity for the Long Island shall offer itself. As I am upon all occasions under the greatest obligations to you, should you get a letter from my son Johnie sooner than I would get one from him, you would very much oblige me by dropping in a few lines communicating to me the most material part of this letter.

I hope you and the ladies of your family will accept of my kindest respects, and I ever am, with esteem,

Dear Madam, your affectionate, humble servant,

FLORA MACDONALD.

P. S.—Please direct to me, to Mrs. Macdonald, late of Kingsborrow, South Uist, by Dunvegan.

To Mrs. Mackenzie of Delvine, by Dunkeld.

The second letter reads:

MILTON, 3RD JULY, 1782.

DEAR MADAM: I received your agreeable favour a fortnight ago, and I am happy to find that your health is not worse than when I left you. I return you my most sincere thanks for your being so mindful of me as to send me the agreeable news about Johny's arrival, which relieved me of a great deal of distress, as that was the first accounts I had of him since he sailed. I think, poor man, he has been very lucky for getting into bread so soon after landing. I had a letter from John which, I suppose, came by the same conveyance with yours. I am told by others that it will be in his power now to show his talents, as being in the engineer's department. He speaks freely of the advantages he got in his youth, and the good example show'd him, which I hope will keep him from doing anything that is either sinful or shameful.

I received a letter from Captain Macdonald, my husband, dated from Halifax, the 12th Nov. '81. He was then recovering his health, but had been very tender for some time before. My son, Charles, is a captain in the British Legion, and James a lieutenant in the same. They are both in New York. Ranald is captain of Marines, and was with Rodney at the taking of St. Eustati. As for my son Sandy, who was amissing, I had accounts of his being carried to Lisbon, but nothing certain, which I look upon, on the whole, as a hearsay; but the kindness of Providence is still to be looked upon, as I have no reason to complain, as God has been pleased to spare his father and the rest. I am now in my brother's house, on my way to Skye, to attend my daughter, who is to ly-in August. They are all in health at present. As for my health at present, it's tolerable, considering my anxious mind and distress at times.

It gives me a great deal of pleasure to hear such good accounts of young Mr. Mackenzie. No doubt he has a great debt to pay who represents his worthy and amiable uncle. I hope you will be so good as remember me to your female companions. I do not despair of the pleasure of seeing you once more, if peace was restored; and I am, dear Madam, with respect and esteem, your affectionate friend,

FLORA MACDONALD.

Having rejoined her husband, immediately after the close of the American Revolution, Flora MacDonald again took up her residence at Kingsburgh house, where she continued to reside until her death, which occurred March 5, 1790, having retained till the last vivacity of character and amiableness of disposition, by which she was distinguished during her whole life. She had gone to a friend's house at Peinduin, in her usual health, to pay a friendly visit, and was there taken suddenly ill with an inflammatory complaint which failed to yield to such medical skill as was available. She retained all her faculties to the last, and calmly departed this life in the presence of her husband and two daughters. Her remains were shrouded in one of the sheets in which Prince Charles had slept at the mansion of Kingsburgh. During all her travels she had never parted with this sheet. She took it with her to North Carolina, and had it in safe keeping when her own person was in danger. At her own request all that was mortal of her was wrapped in it by her sorrowing family. Under shade of night her body was conveyed from Peinduin to Kingsburgh, the coffin being elevated on the shoulders of a party of stalwart youths selected for the purpose. The funeral cortége had proceeded but a

TOMB OF FLORA MACDONALD

The monument is an Iona Cross of the St. Martin Cross type. When erected it was the tallest of the kind in existence, its height being 28½ feet. A gale blew it down and broke off ten feet of it. The inscription around the bevelled edge of the flat stone is in ornamental letters, as follows: "Flora Macdonald born at Milton, South Uist 1722. Died at Kingsburgh Skye 4th Mar. 1790." It was erected by subscription. There is a memorial window to Flora MacDonald in St. Columba Episcopal Church, Portree, Skye.

short distance when it encountered a dreadful storm. The night was of inky darkness, save when relieved by the lightning's red glare. The thunder rolled with terrific peals, and the rain fell in torrents. The Hinisdale was swollen from bank to bank. Some proposed to return, but others declared that she whose body they were carrying had never flinched, when alive, from any duty which she had undertaken, neither would they in performing the last rites to her mortal remains. It was agreed to attempt to cross by the strand near the sea beach, which was effected in safety. Having reached Kingsburgh, the body lay in state for nearly a week. When the day of the funeral arrived several thousand consisting of every rank in Skye and the adjacent isles assembled to pay the last tribute of respect. The procession was a mile in length, and started at an early hour for the church-yard of Kilmuir, at the north end of Skye, sixteen miles distant.

Both Flora's marriage and funeral were the most numerously attended of any in the Western Isles, so far as is known. About a dozen pipers of the schools of MacCrimmon and MacArthur, besides those from other quarters, were present and simultaneously played the "Coronach," the usual melancholy lament for departed greatness.

On September 20, 1795, Allen MacDonald, Seventh of Kingsburgh, departed this life. He is buried by the side of his wife, Flora, who honored him with her heart, and for forty years lavished on him all the wealth and all the generous impulses of a truly noble and generous nature.

Over the grave of his mother, John erected a marble slab, set in a frustom frame, but it was cracked in unloading it from the vessel, and in that state was set up. Within a few months tourists had chipped and carried every particle away. By public subscription a costly monument, with an appropriate inscription, was prepared. It is in the form of an Iona cross, a solid monolith of Aberdeen granite, twenty-eight feet high. This was placed at the grave, but failed to resist the blasts of the northern winds. It was upset and broken in two. It has been partly restored. In Inverness is a monument to Flora's memory. It faces toward the home she loved so well.

To Allen and Flora MacDonald were born ten children, three of whom died in childhood, but names not given. Charles was a captain in MacQueen's Rangers; married, without issue. Alexander, an officer in the Insurrection of the MacDonalds, afterwards in the naval service; went down in the *Ville de Paris,* being on board in command of a prize crew. Never married. Ranald, a captain of marines; unmarried; lost on board the *Ville de Paris.* James served with distinction in Tarleton's Legion; married and had issue. John became Lieutenant-Colonel of the Royal Clan Alpine Regiment, and Commandant of the Royal Edinburgh Artillery; married and had issue. Anne married Major Alexander MacLeod, in 1775, and had issue. In 1834 she died and was buried in her mother's grave. Frances, or Fanny, married Lieutenant Donald MacDonald of Cuidrach, Isle of Skye, with issue.

"Honored be woman, she beams on our sight,
Graceful and fair, like a being of light,
She scatters around her, wherever she strays,
Roses of bliss on our thorn-covered ways—
Roses of Paradise sent from above,
To be gathered and twined in a garland of love."

STATUE OF FLORA MACDONALD ON CASTLE HILL, INVERNESS

This monument was erected at the expense of Capt. T. Henderson MacDonald, a direct descendant of Flora, at a cost of $5,000. It faces Skye. On the front is the inscription, "Fhad's a dh' fhá sas flur air machair Mairidh clui na h-ainnir chaoimh."

Translation of the Gaelic: "As long as a flower grows in field the fame of the gentle lady shall endure."

"The preserver of Prince Charles Edward will be mentioned in history & if courage & fidelity be virtues, mentioned with honour."—Johnson.

APPENDIX

NOTE A.

Since the book went to press I have received a copy of the *Glasgow Weekly Herald,* July 24, 1909, and in it a correspondent relates a recent visit to Kilmuir churchyard, and therein states: "Entering the little graveyard I found myself wading knee-deep amongst coarse weeds and long grasses, with which the whole place—with the exception of a few mounds—was overgrown, giving it an air of sadness and neglect, which even the brilliant sunshine could not dispel. Very few of the old graves had any headstones, and so I stumbled about for a while over the hidden mounds, being unable to tell, amid the tangle, where there was a grave and where there was none. Flora MacDonald's monument stands almost in the center of the little graveyard. It is exposed to all the wild winds of winter, and has at one time been supported on the seaward side by a stout bar of iron; but this now lies detached and useless upon the ground. The great stone, however, looked strong and steadfast, as if determined to defy unaided the wildest storms that blow, and to prove itself a worthy emblem of the brave heart which lies beneath it."

NOTE B.

It may be well to note that the first subscriber to this book is Miss Jessie MacLean, of Greensboro, North Carolina; the second, Mr. Edward L. McClain, of Greenfield, Ohio, and the third, Mr. James A. McAllister, of Lumberton, North Carolina, all of whom have been deeply interested in the enterprise.

DATE DUE